Touched by a Child

GEORGE TOWERY

Touched by a Child

A PRINCIPAL'S STORY

outskirts
press
Denver, Colorado

Touched By A Child, A Principal's Story is dedicated to all of those wonderful students, teachers and families with whom I have had the pleasure of working over the last 45 years.

Contents

Foreword

"We're waiting for Superman." Words uttered by George Towery, and their hollow echo could not ring more true. Education reform has gripped this country with an iron fist and it seems that the more probing questions are asked as to how to "fix" America's public schools, the more obscure and hazy the answers become. As frustrating as this dilemma is, it's glaringly obvious that there isn't one, single, solitary, magic riposte, "Superman," to solve the problem of creating opportunities of adequate education for every student.

So where is Superman? It's about time he swooped down clad in blue tights to save the day, right? Wrong. Despite the common misconceptions, waiting for Superman isn't the problem, because Superman is everywhere. We just don't feel like finding him. Superman is in each of us: That tiny crumb of humanity, that grain of hope, seed of sensitivity. Superman is compassion, and I have yet to meet anyone who embodies compassion better than George Towery.

Compassion! Critics may scoff, politicians may leer, the media may jibe, because, after all, it's the fancy text books and new classrooms, and charter schools that are going to make the difference, right?! Wrong. Compassion is capable of doing exactly the same thing. George Towery was not the principal of a charter school with brand new classrooms or textbooks. Instead he radiated kindness and tolerance to his student body which included many underprivileged kids- the kind of kids people love to stereotype by saying that they won't make it to college, or much less high school graduation. Mr. Towery defied the norm. He created a shelter for many who came from broken homes. He created opportunities for kids that otherwise never would have had such chances. To this day, if you visit my high school and mention the words Cameron Elementary or Mr. Towery, teenagers (yes, sixteen and seventeen year old kids!) faces light up. What they remember is a safe haven. This haven didn't necessarily have a pretty outside, but was filled with loving people on the inside: people who paid no attention to annual income, first languages, or skin color. This school was filled with people who considered one another equals, people who cared. Mr. Towery changed lives, and sometimes it was just by extending an ear and actually listening.

"Knowledge without education is simply information." A once-homeless man told me that, and he had some of the most enlightening ideas on education. He was a man who was educated in the ways of the world. He had seen compassion, and he had witnessed cruelty. He was not ignorant. Did his living condition prompt one to pass judgment? No denying it. But is it an honest evaluation of the problems with education that America's brightest thinkers have fumbled with? Most certainly. What could that cryptic message mean, though? That to learn effectively students must be engaged, interactive, and involved. Otherwise, the knowledge being presented will be diluted into just another statistic. Knowledge needs to be made applicable to real life- it needs to be relevant, or otherwise it will be dismissed. Education is a broad term, and the dictionary defines it as the theory or practice of teaching. Teaching is not preaching, my friends. Teaching is compassion, and namely, compassion, is what will lead to quality edification.

There were maybe six of us slouching on couches in the hot, stuffy, room one Sunday. Mr. Towery sat in front of us and asked, "What's the difference between a preacher and a prophet?" We glanced around at one another lazily, not saying anything. The typical teenage cop-out of "maybe someone else will answer it," definitely crossed our minds. Maybe it was a rhetorical question… or maybe if no one said anything, Mr. Towery would answer it. But he waited patiently, his blue eyes darting from one teenager to the next. He was expecting an answer-damn. Finally someone sputtered out something along the lines of "um… they kinda seem like the same thing…" Mr. Towery smiled. "Oh, but they're not." It was then that he made clear that being a prophet was comparable to teaching while preaching was more like… well, haranguing. Everyone has his or her prophet, he told us. "You know, a role model, someone to look up to, someone who portrays the kind of message that affects you." It was then that he asked us to think of who our prophet was. My mind drew a rather unfortunate blank. Prophet sure seemed like a pretty weighty word. I wouldn't want to deem someone my personal prophet if he or she was unfit! The clock struck ten and the teenagers shuffled out of the Sunday school room. I had yet to speak. It was as Mr. Towery collected his things and started to leave that I looked up and on impulse said, "I think you're my prophet." He paused and looked at me, cocking his head to one side. It was then that some of the most chilling words graced my conscience. "I don't have an answer. I'm not a prophet, Sarah, just a man trying to make a difference."

I gazed back in disbelief, humbled. The man standing before me was someone that I could only aspire to be. He had touched the lives of thousands of kids at their most vulnerable ages, and had sculpted and molded one of the most important things for them: An education. Education is invaluable, and Mr. Towery is someone who made it his priority every day to make sure that an education was out of reach for no one. No exceptions. Never. For him to look at me, and state so blatantly that he was "just trying to make a difference," as if what he were doing was as ordinary as the cereal I'd eaten for breakfast, baffled me. And then he shocked me even further when he said, even more plainly, "It makes me want to do something, but I don't know what- Stick up for these kids is all you can do, I suppose."

Cameron Elementary is (or was) the home for innumerable amounts of kids who recall fondly upon it, with many nostalgic memories. The kids who inhabit(ed) it are a mirror of this country: A country of immigrants, a sea of people all representing different situations, living conditions, and takes on life. This assembly of students is a group susceptible to just about every kind of stereotype, and yet, they were a legion of sorts, striving for a limitless education. Success starts with the basics, a good foundation, and that foundation was a place called Cameron Elementary- a sliver of real life. When I asked Mr. Towery why he decided to write this book, he looked at me and made the kind of unbreakable eye contact that makes you feel like he's probing into your soul, searching your being. "Because you don't find their kind of character just everywhere. They're beautiful children; people just need to know," he said. "They just need to know. That's all." His gaze flickered and then he stared back, with an even hotter intensity than before.

"You see a lot of things in these kids that we've almost lost in this country: a caring for one another- compassion." I smiled, George Towery had nailed it.

I apologize, I never introduced myself. I'm a sophomore in high school. In the relative scheme of things, I know nothing. Ignorance is bliss right? Ehh, I disagree. This book, this memoir, which Mr. Towery has assembled for you, is years of memories and experiences compiled into a tidy stack of pages laden with words. Words that will educate, because ignorance is only a setback to understanding one another. These words will take each of you on a journey, because if I know anything about Mr. Towery, it's that he can tell a story. His stories will appeal to your sensibilities. He will send shivers down your spine as you realize the harsh realities of life, or release butterflies in the pit of your stomach as those shards of such simple happiness make you grin. Best of luck, reader, because what you're about to partake in is going to change your view on education, kids, people, life, the human condition.

Sarah King
Edison High School

Introduction

For more than a few years, the Nation's schools have been blamed for the ills of our society. If the schools would have just "done it right" all of the problems facing our society would have been lessened, even long ago eliminated. We've tried grants, a multitude of reading, math and science programs, technology and teacher pay for performance. No Child Left Behind followed to simply proclaim that by 2013 every child in the United States would read on grade level regardless of background, native language or learning ability. The attempt to put all children, all schools and all teachers in the same pot, stir it and have everything and everybody come out looking alike was nothing short of foolish. Given the preceding scenario, it is interesting that teachers have traditionally been some of the most revered individuals in our society. When asked, "Who was the most influential person in your life beside your parents?" folks almost always name a teacher. In spite of the criticism, teachers and schools continue to make a huge difference in people's lives every day of every year.

The foundation of good schools has always been good teachers. Capable, well trained, caring teachers who work together along with outstanding administrators were and continue to be the bottom line. Schools have always been strictly a people business though at times we've paid less than adequate attention to that. Modern, well equipped buildings were thought to be necessary, comfortable, and even motivational. However, in spite of their beauty, functionality and first class equipment, buildings have never been a match for the quality of those who worked inside. Having served as principal in both antiquated and modern buildings, except for creature comforts, the quality of the program was and is still determined by the people. A staff of outstanding teachers is only the first step toward a quality education program. Staff, to be effective, must possess the ability to work, collaborate with and support colleagues in order to reach out daily and establish quality relationships with all youngsters; relationships based on trust, love and a passion for teaching.

Several years ago I saw an advertisement for a book entitled Children Don't Work for Teachers They Don't Like. I didn't purchase the book, but the title stuck with me. Over the years that title has often impacted my thinking as I worked with staff to plan not only the best academic program for youngsters but one that would encourage, inspire and motivate as well. Through my 40 years as an elementary principal I have too often met concerned, well-prepared teachers, professionals, who for whatever reason lacked the ability to reach out to youngsters and become significant characters in their lives. As a result, these well meaning teachers failed to motivate students to achieve to the fullest. All the planning, all the hard work, the sincerest effort was met with less than spectacular results when they were unable to create a classroom or a school environment that not only instructed but inspired and motivated our children: Indeed a school or classroom where learning flourished and where each child knew they were special and important.

I remember some years ago at a conference listening to a school superintendent speak and state emphatically that every child in his district would learn to read. I have often thought since that it was sad he stopped there and failed to include that every child in the district would like to read or choose to read or want to read. If we lose sight of the joy of learning, we have "missed the boat." Often these days it seems our task has become little more than teaching the basic reading, writing, math, science and social studies skills in order to prove by a test score that the children in our schools achieve.

Today's schools are not just factories producing little learners, achievers and test scores. Schools are much more than that. In schools we still sow the seeds for the future of our world, mold the attitudes of the next generation and bring creativity, individuality and thinking into modern day. We do this both in sane and insane ways. As teachers and principals we conjure up all sorts of motivational gimmicks, "tricks of the trade," and become clowns, TV stars, acrobats, whatever seems necessary to get learning across. Think about your own education and your teachers. Think about those individuals who were able to broaden your horizons, expand your then known world well beyond the classroom and guide you on unfamiliar paths. Their classrooms were happy, buzzing with the excitement of learning, sometimes in unconventional ways.

Too often yet, the public schools of our Nation are made to

be the "whipping boy" of society. Our most outspoken critics are often those affluent, wealthy individuals who can afford to send their children to private schools and employ tutors so that their children can gain admission to top rated colleges and universities. Indeed, some public schools, especially in our inner cities, are in trouble for a variety of reasons that are very real and include violence, poverty and the absence of family. However, even in those schools, there are scores of dedicated, hard working teachers and principals who continue, in spite of criticism and the lack of resources, to make huge differences in the lives of our Nation's youngsters, rich and poor, black, white, Asian and Latino in classrooms every single day.

Both of the schools in which I served as principal had student populations from across all financial strata including significant numbers of youngsters from impoverished situations, different cultures and widely varied backgrounds. The schools were identified as Title 1 schools, a label given those schools with a high percentage of students from low socio-economic situations. Early on I thought I wanted to open a new school in my career, but my wife was quick to remind me that was not likely to happen, because new schools weren't built in the communities in which I chose to work. She was right; I found my niche.

My experiences as principal dealt not only with education, but with the basics of life, even survival. The daily routine of the school was often interrupted in surprising and unexpected ways. Each child came to school with his or her own story. Their stories had a profound effect on each of us and begged to be shared, heard, and understood. Similar stories occur daily in schools like ours all across the country. In the pages that follow, you will find the stories of our children as well as joys, disappointments and lessons learned over the last forty years. In attempting to manage two of those complicated, yet very special, institutions that we call school, I was given the opportunity to touch young lives. Far more than that, countless wonderful children touched my life and that of each person on the staff every day.

Reflections on a Big Yellow Bus

Looking back, I remember sitting in my office realizing that a perpetual line formed outside the door to see me. I never believed that I was worth waiting in line for. Obviously, the folks out there felt quite differently. Some were speaking loudly, enough to make certain that I knew there was a line and hoping that I would move along and get to them quickly. Mrs. Rojas was there to get a letter to take to immigration verifying that her children were in school and what grades they were in. Mrs. Jackson, fifth grade teacher, was crying, dealing with elderly parents half way across the country and knowing that she would need time off. Susie, a second grader, brought a cupcake for me because it was her birthday and it was important to her that she hand it to me personally. Mr. Ramad was waiting to tell me that his family was returning to their home country, Ethiopia, for three weeks and wanting to know if his children would be excused. It was early morning on a typical day.

As I tried to focus my attention on each of the needs brought to me; in the back of my mind I was aware that I had a classroom observation in fifteen minutes. I knew that if I were late, increased pressure would be upon the teachers as they had prepared carefully, wanting to make certain that all went well and knowing that they would have to keep the children busy until I arrived. On the corner of my desk I saw the Title 1 budget for our school that was not complete yet due that day. I tried to avoid glancing toward the computer screen because I really didn't want to know how many emails were waiting and of those how many expected an immediate response. It was also the end of the month and the secretary was reminding me that we needed our monthly fire drill. This would be a good day because the weather was going to be nice.

If I could just have spent a little more time in the classes with the children, my days would have been made. The children were ever welcoming. They were anxious for you to see the power point presentation they had completed, read their essay, look at the 100% they received on their math test, or just listen as they read hoping that you would praise their progress. In kindergarten I was like some kind of hero as at the beginning of the year every kindergarten teacher would tell those just beginning their educational career, "I want you to meet someone special, this is Mr. Towery, HE'S THE PRINCIPAL." After that kind of introduction, a visit to any one of the kindergarten classes could only make you feel like a real star and you would leave with at least one piece of five year old art work, paste everywhere, promising you would put it on your office door so they could see it when they came by. Visits in classrooms with the children were never tiring, always fun and often included some surprises like, "Mommy had daddy arrested last night," or "My big brother wrecked the car."

As principal, I never considered myself a hero, much less a star. I was often overwhelmed just knowing how many people were dependent upon me. I listened, offered approval, encouragement, and at times criticism. The line outside my door was almost always there expecting a thoughtful response, advice, reassurance for whatever need existed at that moment. They knew that I would have the right answer though I was far less certain of that than they. Staff knew that one of my tasks was to evaluate them and that I would do all I could to make their job easier and them more effective. Don't I wish I could have made every teacher as GREAT as each would have liked to become. Parents believed that I had the power to do the right thing for each of their children as they learned and grew. I only wish I had known all of "the right things" to do. The children saw me as a guide, helper and friend, one who knew what to do to solve their problems. I so hope that what I did made a difference, even if just a tiny bit for each of them.

In meetings and in the literature we were frequently reminded that the principal is the leader and sets the tone for the school; an awesome task. The needs were never ending. There was always something important to do. There was never a boring or even slightly dull day. I knew that a significant part of the lives of these little ones were in my hands. I worked to do the best for them because I knew each was striving to become a capable and productive citizen. I realized that this was the most important job I could ever do. How did I have the good fortune to be so blessed? I pondered. What led me to this place, this opportunity? As a child growing up what were the influences that prompted me to end up here? Perhaps a major one came in a most unexpected way.

As I hit my teen age years I was anxious to drive. Indeed, I could hardly wait. My parents allowed me to learn as soon as I was of age. In Virginia, at that time, you could get your driver's license at fifteen. I was a high school sophomore. We had only one car, which was customary for families, so there was no way that I could even think about driving to school. Along with every other high school student in the neighborhood, I rode the school bus daily. Mrs. Louise Vanderver was our bus driver. As I got on the bus at the first stop and off at the last, I got to know Mrs. Vanderver rather well. She seemed to enjoy driving the yellow monster and putting up with all of us "charming" kids.

At that time, along with the adult bus drivers, many of the school bus drivers were high school students. It was a wonderful part time job. The pay was $100 a month. You got to take the vehicle home, you didn't have to stand at the bus stop in bad weather, and the other students in the neighborhood loved the convenience. I couldn't wait. I was determined to learn to drive a school bus.

Can you imagine today if the school bus drivers were high school students? There would be protests, lawsuits, complaints, etc. and most parents would drive their children to school. In the late 1950's student bus drivers were not uncommon. Mrs. Vanderver, with the blessing of the school system, was allowed to instruct me. After passing the test, I became a school bus driver mid-way through my junior year in high school. As a beginner, I was given bus #22, the oldest bus that the school system had that was still operational. It was an "International" mid- 1940's vintage. I had three bus routes that took me to elementary, middle and high school. My first period at school was my free period and my high school was the first dismissed in the afternoon.

None of the buses had power steering or automatic transmission. Neither did they have heaters that worked very well. I wonder now how I learned to drive as the bus was an antique; old, creaky and difficult to steer or stop. The worst was the transmission that had to be "double clutched" every time you shifted gears. That meant when you went from one gear to the next, you pushed the clutch in and moved the shifter to neutral, let it out, pushed the clutch in again and moved the shifter to the next gear. That was bad enough, but going uphill with a bus loaded with students you had to go down through the gears in the same manner adding an additional step when you got to neutral. It took me a while to master that.

Still, I must have been considered a safe and responsible driver. Within a few weeks I received a much newer bus that was like a Cadillac compared to the older one. My old #22 was passed on to the next newest driver. I was in heaven. No high school student could have been more ecstatic than I, sitting behind the wheel of a slick vehicle capable of carrying 66 passengers. The only ones not so ecstatic were my parents who did not mind me driving the bus. However, they weren't too happy having the big bright yellow thing sitting in front of our suburban home in the evenings and on weekends.

The start of my senior year brought a wonderful surprise. I was assigned a new school bus, a big V-8 Ford, with a huge, flat hood and a loud muffler. Everything this high school student ever wanted. Now I had power and the muffler to let others know that I was coming. I also had a heater that was much improved. My senior year in high school was perfect.

As I drove the bus I really developed wonderful relationships with the students: Elementary, middle and high school and the staffs of the individual schools as well. The student passengers seemed to enjoy me as much as I enjoyed them. I was careful but always had a good time. I remember the day that Alan Shephard became the first man in space, May 5, 1961, in the Mercury 7 space capsule. The steering went out on the bus as we were on our way to school in front of Scotty D'Angelo's house, and we all poured into his living room to watch the historic event on television. Later in the day, the school system sent a substitute bus, and we went on to school.

On another day, with a load of high school students, a Holmes bread truck was blocking the road. The delivery man, when he saw the school bus, raced down the driveway, jumped into the truck and took off. As he did the back doors flew open and several trays of donuts and pastries fell out. The students hopped off the bus and rescued those donuts and pastries. To a bunch of high school students on their way to school it was nothing short of an absolute feast.

As my high school graduation day approached, I had been accepted to Wake Forest College, now University. However, it was with mixed emotion that I gave up my school bus. The last day of school the parents of my elementary students threw a big party decorating the interior of the bus, providing lots of goodies, "Thank You's" and Congratulations. What a happy ending! Thanks to my experience with the big yellow school bus, I went off to college knowing that I had been successful working with kids and knowing that my destiny was to become a teacher.

Four years later, standing in front of my own sixth grade class was nothing short of a dream come true. I had worked to prepare and now it was real. Like every beginning teacher, I thought I knew far more than I did, was going to solve every child's problem, have every child on grade level and meet every parent's expectations. While being in front of the class every day was a thrill, I soon learned that my expectations of myself were not always realistic. I could not solve every child's problem. What I could do was my very best every day to see that the students learned, understood and had the opportunity to think, create and expand their knowledge. I was determined to make certain the students knew they were appreciated, cared for and were treated with respect.

What I learned:

- **You never know what experience in life is going to guide your path.**
- **Students are fun regardless of age.**
- **Driving a big yellow bus will get you recognized in the neighborhood.**
- **To a seventeen year old in 1960, $ 100 a month was a fantastic salary.**
- **Teaching is never boring, neither will you ever run out of something important to do.**

Me, A Principal?

I was not long into the classroom when the words "Masters Degree" came up. "George, you had better begin to work on your Masters," Mrs. Johns, our principal, would say. "It will be easier for you to get it now before you have a family of your own than it will be later." I was strongly advised that as a man, I needed to get my degree in administration so I would have the opportunity to make a larger salary, especially if I expected to be a father and have children of my own. I heeded the advice and began to work on my Masters Degree the second semester of my first year. As far as seeking an endorsement in administration, that was too far off to even think about. While I liked the idea of more money, at that point I was not seriously interested in becoming a principal.

I worked on my degree in the evening and lived on campus at the University of Virginia during the summer. At school I worked daily at becoming a more effective teacher. I soon learned that I worked well with those students who had problems, especially in terms of their behavior. They were often sent or delivered to my class during the school day and they always wanted to stay once there. Not that I was so terribly strict, indeed I thought I was a pushover. I just liked the kids and was able to establish sincere and respectful relationships. They responded well and gave their best for me in terms of their work.

I remember working with one student, Bobby Kaminski, who could not get his behavior under control. Unlike others who just liked to talk, not focus on learning or disrupt, Bobby would lie and steal almost daily. No one, kids or adults, wanted him around as he could not be trusted. I went to Mrs. Johns and told her that I simply could not work with Bobby any longer, I was getting nowhere, and she might need to move him somewhere else. I was shocked by her response when rather than agreeing with me, she told me that in my career I would have more than one Bobby and as a teacher it was my job to find strategies that would encourage and motivate him. I never referred another student to the office and indeed worked with Bobby. That was a powerful lesson for me and impacted the rest of my career. Being a teacher or principal was not just about those students who were easy to work with, but the difficult ones as well. The last time I saw Bobby he pulled into my home driveway in an expensive sports car, thanked me for all I had done for him and announced that he was a successful lawyer in Birmingham, Alabama.

My last year as a classroom teacher I had about twenty-five boys in an "all boys" class. They had an assortment of problems, many of those academic, others behavioral. A quarter of them had repeated a grade somewhere along the way and some were just not interested in school. It was a successful year for both them and me. At the end, their reward for a job well done was a weekend camping trip, my first of many camping trips with kids. Students and parents together were excited as we pitched tents, untangled fishing lines and cooked over an open fire. The boys went on to seventh grade much happier than when they had arrived. I knew they were a little more motivated, successful academically and interested in school. One student, Dr. Frank Murphy, still keeps in close contact with me to this day, 40+ years later. As a physician in North Carolina, I see him at least annually on his trips to this area.

Prior to the end of my fourth year, I had earned my Masters Degree. Mrs. John's was regularly pushing me to become a principal and I had worked closely enough with her to begin to realize exactly what the responsibilities of a principal were. During the last weeks of the school year as I dismissed students at the end of the day, I noticed a man outside my classroom door whom I did not know. He introduced himself as Dr. J. Michael Davidson, Area Superintendent. He proceeded to tell me that there was an opening for assistant principal at a neighboring elementary school and that I should make an appointment to talk to the principal. I was totally surprised as I had done nothing to seek an administrative position. Further, I was so naive that I thought he was offering me the job. I soon found out that I was one of the candidates who had been contacted.

Realizing that this was an excellent opportunity and knowing that someone had enough faith in me to believe I could do the job, I decided to visit the school. I did as I was instructed; called, made an appointment, and met Sarah Miller, the principal. Mrs. Miller and I struck up a good friendship at the first meeting and I left feeling like I would be offered the position. I was right.

As our suburban school system was opening new schools every few months at that time, assistant principals remained one year before becoming principals. My year with Mrs. Miller was a pleasure, the two of us developed a wonderful relationship and I soaked up everything she tried to teach me. Needless to say, I learned a lot and I think assisted Mrs. Miller as well.

Sure enough, at the end of the year I was summoned to the Superintendent's office along with two other assistants who I knew well. We went into the brief meeting together and each of us was given our new assignment as principal. No one asked us if we had applied. Neither were we asked if we wanted the assignment. We left somewhat stunned, albeit excited, anxious to return to our schools and share the news.

What I learned:

- Teaching is a wonderful career choice.
- Pursuing a Masters Degree early in my career was a wise thing.
- Motivation is an important part of the job for every educator, even with the most difficult students.
- When opportunity knocks, don't hesitate.

Lorton

In August of 1970 two months before my 27th birthday, now married with one young son and another well on the way, I walked into Lorton Elementary School as the new principal. The school, built in 1934, was old and outdated for our rapidly growing suburban school system. Young, first-time principals don't begin in new, modern buildings. Earlier in the spring the school had been burned by vandals leaving everything beyond the end of the main hallway boarded up including the cafeteria, kitchen and a number of classrooms. Pending a quick insurance settlement and subsequent reconstruction; a newer wing, and a few classrooms in the existing building were the only areas accessible to staff and students. With 600 students expected in a month, it looked like there would be many classes in temporary classrooms when school opened.

The building, in a then rural area of the county, bordered Interstate 95, constructed some 20 years after the school had been built. As a result, the east side of the building sat 100 yards from the highway, separated only by a seven foot high chain link fence. Nothing would be quiet, especially in warm weather. I was certain that I could expect many complaints from teachers, especially those in trailers and on that side of the building.

The school also sat less than a mile from a large reformatory serving prisoners from the District of Columbia known as "Lorton." In its prime, the prison had been a source of pride and employment in the community. It was far away from the City with carefully manicured lawns, white picket fences around staff housing, a large dairy and carefully maintained buildings. With the coming of the highway, the facility seemed suddenly only a few miles from DC, now easily accessible and a quick trip by car. The pride had been diminished, the fences were gone. The reformatory was perceived to be poorly managed and had become a part of the community that everyone now wished no longer existed. Indeed, the reformatory had kept development away from that corner of the county. The reformatory was destined to become both a blessing and a curse in my new role.

In the small main office I met the secretary, Mrs. Norma Rhodes. Sitting behind a large counter, she was a wrinkled lady easily old enough to be my mother. She promptly told me that she had lived in the Lorton community all her life, knew everyone in the community and had been the school secretary for more than 20 years. She also told me that her three grandchildren attended the school and that she kept a close eye on them and expected me to do the same. Further, she was very surprised that one as young as I could become principal. I determined that I had better stay out of her way as much as possible and certainly do everything I could not to get on her "bad" side. I realized that I needed all of the help I could get.

My office was tiny with the ceiling height being the greatest dimension in the room. It consisted of a desk, desk chair and two cushion bright green vinyl covered couch. My desk had been completely cleared of everything, paper clips, pencils, etc. except for a large wooden paddle which I soon learned that I was expected to use on occasion. My classroom teaching experience in a middle class school with a loving older woman principal did not prepare me for a paddle which I assumed she would never have thought of using nor would have I. Fortunately, the school system prohibited paddling just a year or two after I became principal.

August is hot in the Washington area and so was my office. There was no air conditioning anywhere in the building though new schools were being built with air conditioning at the time. I convinced my wife that as a result of my promotion to principal, we should put central air conditioning in our house so that I could take the window unit in our bedroom and install it in my new office. She agreed, and I installed my first air conditioner only to realize that I was ashamed to sit in my office and work with the door closed while Mrs. Rhodes sat outside of my door sweating from the heat. I managed to find a used larger window unit and a friend to install the upgraded wiring so that it would work. That certainly did not hurt my relationship with Mrs. Rhodes and seemed to begin to bring the school into the 20th century.

As the summer progressed, I was fortunate to get to know my self-appointed, yet wonderful mentor, supporter and guide, Mrs. Leslie Hammond. A long time principal, who loved her job, she knew the "ins and outs" of the system and the job. Leslie was principal at my neighboring school, and had also been raised in the Lorton community in a house immediately adjacent to my school. A second older, wrinkled woman with a definite toughness, she walked with a severe limp from having had polio as a child and away from the kids was seldom without her unfiltered Camel cigarette. Leslie obviously had the respect and admiration of our school system as well as the community. With some stake in the Lorton community, there was no way that she was going to let me fail at my new task. Not only was she quick to say, "Well done," she was just as quick to say, "You had better not try that," or "You had better do that over." Her continuing support, listening ear and encouragement not only made my first year more pleasant but helped me fully understand the job of principal and what was expected of me. I became a better principal because of her.

As I was not quite twenty-seven years old, most of the staff were older than I, some much older, some even old enough to be my parent. How was I to address my new staff? In casual conversation was it best to say, Mr. Nelson and Mrs. Smith, or simply Bill and Mary. First names became easy for the younger staff, but for the older staff it was Mr. and Mrs. or Miss. Finally our librarian, likely the oldest teacher on staff said, "Look, George, I am Esther, just Esther. When you call me Mrs. Cranford and everyone else Mary or Bill you set me apart. I appreciate your effort to be courteous but we are all in this together." After that, it was strictly first names. We worked through the summer, met delightful teachers, parents and students, opened school in cramped quarters and were off and running.

Shortly after the opening of school, the school system settled with the insurance company and reconstruction of the building began. Not only would we get a beautifully modified building but a small classroom addition, a music room for the first time, a cafeteria that would double as a gymnasium, new ceilings throughout. All of the reconstructed area would be air conditioned. I was thrilled!! By the opening of school my second year, reconstruction was completed, the community was proud and I was given much of the credit for the now beautifully reconstructed area. My standing in the community certainly improved even though I had done nothing to earn that. The word was out that Principal Towery gets things done.

What I learned:

- When things are bad, there is only one way to go and that's up.
- Perception is reality.
- If people think you have done something for their benefit then you have done it indeed.
- Little things like an air conditioned office can really improve a relationship.
- A secretary who is old enough to be your mother who knows the community and tells everyone what you are doing is not a bad thing.
- To do the principal's job well, a good mentor is essential at the beginning.
- It's not the building but the people who make the school.

Weary Travelers and the Auto Train

As I assumed the position of principal, I envisioned my role would be to do everything in my power to see that all students had the best possible educational opportunities to achieve and meet their academic potential. Sounds good!!

In the beginning, I did not realize that the principal's job description was like a blank sheet. There was nothing, no, nothing that the principal could not do. If Julie was hysterical because she knew her mom would "kill her" because she accidentally threw her retainer away while disposing of her lunch, guess what; I helped Julie hunt for the retainer. If Jose threw up everywhere, the custodian was not around, everyone else was gagging and the classroom was in turmoil as a result, I became "Johnny on the Spot." If tearful first grade Brett had diarrhea, messed all over himself and the bathroom, no one was anxious to deal with it so I stepped in, cleaned him up, found clean clothes for him to put on then called mom. Perhaps one of my most difficult tasks during those first few years was entering a first grade classroom to inform the teacher that her house was on fire and in turn driving her home to see all of the fire apparatus and the flames coming out of her home.

At Lorton, because of our proximity to Interstate 95, I quickly became aware that in addition to all of our other duties, we would daily be called upon to provide travel information and a rest stop to countless hundreds of travelers. I did not think that so many folks would or could become lost in their travels or that our school building could be mistaken for a train station or a rest stop. But, Lorton was the first exit south of the City that looked to be simple to exit and return to the highway, so people stumbled on us easily.

In spite of our efforts to require visitors to first report to the office, travelers, most often elderly, would wander in, down the halls, into the office or into the classrooms and inquire about rest rooms, a place to eat lunch or simply seek travel information. I was always amazed that they would just as soon talk to a third grader as an adult, expecting that accurate information would be given. Actually, it was often quite funny and we ended up laughing at the events of the day. One lady who came in said, "I was going from Silver Spring to Oxon Hill (Maryland), where in the hell am I?" I replied, "You are in the wrong state, Mam. You are in Lorton, Virginia." At that point she threw her hands over her chest and exclaimed, "Oh my God, do you think they will kill me (meaning the prisoners at the reformatory)." My response was, "Well, they haven't killed us yet." We gave her directions, and she went on her way. We laughed.

On one occasion a very elderly couple from Asbury Park, New

Jersey, came into the office in sheer panic. They were on their way to Florida. The lady did all of the driving because the husband was far too feeble to drive. They had stopped "Up the road" to buy gas and she had left her pocketbook containing all of their money, her driver's license and papers in the gas station rest room. Neither of them knew how far "Up the road" was, what exit from the highway they had taken, or even the brand of gasoline they had purchased. We did our best to calm them down but really could offer little other than a kind word without any specific information. We called the police for them, and thankfully the officer who arrived was very gentle and kind. After a while they were on their way back "Up the road" to try to locate the gas station where they had stopped. We often wondered if they ever got to Florida or even back to Asbury Park.

Yet another time some poor senior had to use the bathroom so badly that as the car pulled up she quickly hopped out, pulled down her panties and urinated right there in the parking lot with kids laughing and people saying, "Did you see that?" One day a young male teacher was leaving to go home only to discover that his car had been propped up on cinderblocks with all four wheels missing. Someone really needed a set of tires and no one had seen a thing. The perils of being close to the Interstate.

Our 1970's community of Lorton was still a rather rural area of our county. The intersection at Interstate 95 seemed quite simple to us. It consisted of four corners. When you exited Interstate 95 the corner on your right was empty, directly across the road was the school. As you turned left and passed under the highway there was a Shell gas station on the right corner and the Auto Train terminal on the left. That was it. Yet, seemingly no one could find the Auto Train. On older lady entered the front door one day to remark, "Are all of these children going on the Auto Train?" I guess if that were to be the case she was considering changing her mind. Frequently folks would arrive early for Amtrak's Auto Train from Lorton to Sanford, Florida which began to board about two o'clock in the afternoon.

We supplied a variety of other services and became a popular lunch spot as there was no where else to eat in the area. Our cafeteria staff was always welcoming and glad to serve them. In the 1970's we did all of our cooking at the school. You could smell bread baking throughout the building, other sweet aromas and could get quite a nice lunch for a couple of dollars. This worked well except for the day that an older woman became quite irate that she could not buy a mixed drink. We reminded her that this was a school and obviously couldn't serve alcohol. We were doing her a service by letting her eat at all.

The Auto Train passengers were happy to sit in the cafeteria, eat with and talk to the kids who always responded kindly to the older adults. On our sixth grade trip to New York as we prepared to board the Statue of Liberty ferry, our students, in their "Lorton Lions" tee shirts were greeted by a kind gentleman who said, "I've been to your school." Students were pleased that this regular Auto Train passenger could identify them several hundred miles from home.

One retired New Jersey primary school teacher made the round trip to Florida every fall and returned in the spring. She would make it a point to arrive very early going both north and south so that she could spend the day with the students. She was eager to visit the primary classrooms, read to the students and assist the teacher in any way she could. She always thanked us for letting her come and would send a note to the teacher after her visit. Once a teacher, always a teacher!

Almost every one of our students was transported to school by bus. When the interstate was constructed, Gunston Cove Road ran beside the gas station on the other side of the highway. Three or four of our students lived on rural Gunston Cove Road, a light industrial area, and could walk to school. All others were transported on school buses. A walking tunnel under the highway was built at the end of our school driveway for that purpose, and they used it daily. Most of the Auto Train folks seemed quite well off financially. They drove Cadillac's, Mercedes and other large, expensive cars. One day a couple came in for directions to the train. We told them to go out to the road, go under the highway, and they would see the station on the left. They went out and we glanced to see that they were going the right way. Instead of going out on the main road, they remained in our school driveway. We observed that the man would drive up to the walking tunnel and back up. He did this repeatedly a number of times. Shortly thereafter, he came back into the office and stated, "I don't know what kind of car you drive, but mine will not go through that road." We got them turned around, and I hope they found the train a block away.

When Hurricane Agnes came through Northern Virginia in June of 1972, school had just closed for the year. Parts of the interstate were completely submerged, bridges going south were washed out, and travelers were stranded. I arrived at school the next morning to find a parking lot full of cars that had been towed to our school: cars that had been under water on the Interstate and were completely ruined. I also found families camping on the front lawn in tents and pop up trailers anxious for someone to arrive so that they had access to restrooms and basic facilities. We spent the day assisting travelers, the police and highway departments getting folks on their way, providing meals to the stranded and a place to rest. Because our boiler room had also flooded as a result of Agnes, the county maintenance department called early in the day and asked me to, "Run down to the boiler room and turn the main power off before the custodian goes down there and electrocutes himself." I was startled to learn that, in his eyes custodians were more valuable than principals. Actually, when he realized what he had said, he immediately apologized and said that he wished me no harm. Until the water receded, no one went down in the boiler room.

What I learned:

- **People cannot easily follow even the simplest directions in a car.**
- **There are lots of folks driving on our highways who shouldn't be.**
- **The principal's job is much more than I reckoned it to be and I hadn't yet come close to seeing it all.**

Pohick Estates to Seven Hills

Violet's family emigrated to Lorton from the hills of eastern Kentucky as unskilled laborers anxious to make a better living in the big city. Daniel's father was a county firefighter, and his mother a hair dresser. Julie's dad was a respected corporate lawyer in Washington. That was the diversity in our community. In most suburban or urban school communities the populations of a particular school come from similar backgrounds. Lorton was a natural community with folks from all walks of life coming together to see that their children were given the best opportunity to learn and grow. Those who had nothing worked, played and learned with those who were privileged and neither was bothered by it. When Bessie had her birthday even though her house had no indoor plumbing, the children of the rich were invited and attended. Students developed remarkable relationships and respect for each other.

In many middle class communities families tried to move up the ladder of success. They were involved with the PTA, Little League, etc. They demanded the best for their children because they felt that each was gifted and brighter than all others in the school. Often they gave teachers a rough time trying to meet their demands. Those families that had little or nothing simply appreciated all that was done for their children, thanked you repeatedly and willingly shared what they had. Those who were already privileged knew that they did not need to impress and saw the school as an opportunity for learning and for life.

Our poorer children resided in the more rural areas of the community. Most families came from Appalachia, southwest Virginia or eastern Kentucky. English often seemed a second language as their fast spoken dialects made it difficult at times for us to understand what they were saying. Their houses were being built by their fathers and their neighbors. They lived in them as is, and when there was enough money, they finished another room. Often unfinished, the outside was always made to look better than the inside.

I visited Rebecca's house one day. She had ugly sores on her face which needed to be addressed medically, and we were unable to contact her family as there was no phone. As I pulled up to the house I was impressed by the rather stately looking home with two stories, pink siding and white shutters. When the mother opened the door, I was taken aback and realized that the front of the house was all that was complete. The inside was nothing but studs where the walls and rooms were to eventually be. As I left I made a point to look back at the side of the house to see that sheets of exposed plywood covered the sides. That is what you call, "putting on a good front."

One fall night when the time was to change from Daylight Savings Time back to Eastern Standard Time, I received a call from Rebecca's father. There had been some sort of problem at school. Since her father was waiting up until 2 a.m. to change his clock, that's when he called me. I was asleep. He figured that if he was up, I was as well. He was very surprised that one as smart as I had not remembered to stay up to change my clock. In my sleepy state I did not try to explain that one does not really need to stay up until 2 a.m. to change the clock back an hour.

So many homes were without plumbing, or on antiquated septic systems. Though there was always electricity, homes were often heated by wood stoves. I had occasion to visit Sammy's, a very small and frail first grader, who had not been coming to school. I arrived to find him in the dirt of the front yard holding what appeared to be a very dead rat. Momma came out and spoke with me indicating that she would do her best to get Sammy to come to school and that sometimes he "just didn't want to go." I learned during my visit that Sammy had a younger brother who slept in a crib while Sammy slept in the bath tub. Of course, there was no plumbing in the house at that time so the tub was a logical place for him to sleep. The family looked forward to the time when they could complete their bath room.

We were almost never invited into many of their homes because they were embarrassed by how little they had and did not want us to see their unfinished homes. It was not uncommon to hear that Susie did not come to school because she had no shoes or that the children had to go home and gather kindling for the stove. Countless committed and loving teachers regularly took money out of their own pockets so kids could have shoes, socks, underwear or school supplies, the things that seemed to be most lacking.

Our middle class kids came from a large subdivision called Pohick Estates. Families were high school and college educated and almost all of them very supportive of the school and school staff. To visit a home in Pohick Estates was very different than visiting one of the homes in the poorer areas. Families were almost always flattered that you would visit, invited you in, and often offered you a cup of coffee. We considered those families the mainstay of our community. Indeed the greatest percentage of our students came from Pohick Estates. Those families were among our greatest supporters.

The other area of our community included the five acre estates in the far western part of our attendance area. Those homes did not have a Lorton post office address but that of Fairfax Station which was far more prestigious. We found the families most gracious, supportive of and interested in the school. My wife and I were invited to a community Christmas party at one of the homes and observed that our entire home, which we did not consider small, would fit entirely in their living room. Those families as well were very attentive to those with needs and repeatedly advised us to call on them if we found particular needs in the community.

One interesting family, the Washington's, lived on the corner of one of the estate communities. The Washington's were an African American family with five boys. Although you could not see their house from the road, the family lived in what we would today call a shack, built no telling when. Mrs. Washington would often and proudly tell you that was her property, given to her ancestors when the slaves were freed from one of the local farms. We assumed it was true. Certainly they did own the property and I don't know how else they could have purchased it. I often thought what it must be like for those boys to ride the bus home with the other children all of whom were going to large and stately homes when they were going to a ramshackle place that had little or nothing.

Everyone knew and looked after the boys and momma at school, making certain that they had clothes and groceries. When the time came for Mike, the middle son, to go to middle school, he did not want to leave, however, there was no reason not to promote him. Several months into seventh grade the principal of the large secondary school called me and said that Mike was not doing well. All he wanted every day was to come back to Lorton. What did I think of the idea? We agreed that if Mike wanted to come that badly it was fine. Mike had a great second sixth grade year and went on the following year without problems. There was no substitute for knowing that you were appreciated loved and cared for, and Mike was.

Some of our areas were difficult to access by school bus and kids had to walk to the main road. The streets were dead ends or there was no good place for the bus to turn around. There were never any sidewalks. Lorfax Heights was such a place. Kids had a long walk to the bus stop and had to stand along the main road. We tried and tried to get the bus to go into Lorfax Heights but were repeatedly told that there were no through streets and that the bus was not allowed to back up and turn around. Thus it remained. In our estate communities, however, a prominent family with political connections moved in and the very next day, the bus went in to the estate community backed up and turned around twice. Money does talk.

On another occasion the school system made a major push to see that students attended the school in their home attendance area. For whatever reason you positively would not, could not or should not attend a school outside of the area where you lived. It happened that the daughter of an influential family was cared for by another influential family in one of our large estate communities. The child's mother cried and tried without success to have her daughter continue at Lorton because they had moved to another school attendance area and she was comfortable with her child care arrangement. One morning the Superintendent of our large school system called me. Superintendent's never called. I thought, "Oh my God, what have I done." When I got to the phone, he said, "George, you know Mrs. Collins who wants her daughter at your school. Let the child come and don't you dare tell one damn soul that I told you to do it." We complied and up until now I have never told.

In the 1970's, everything in the community was overshadowed by fear of and anger toward the reformatory. Prison breaks were common. The Lorton community was a recurring headline in the "Washington Post" and on the local television. Students and staff became used to the announcement over the loudspeaker stating that we were locking down. It was not necessary to say why, because everyone knew there was a prison break. The kids grumbled not because the doors were all locked but because there was no outdoor recess that day. On more than one occasion we had guards with guns in the front of our school when it was known that escapees were in our immediate area. On another occasion one of our families, the Bradley's, were held hostage in their home by several convicts who had escaped. Our best friend became one of the parents, Mrs. Waymon, who was the switch board operator at the reformatory. I am certain that at times we received a call from her announcing a prison break before some of the reformatory staff was even aware. Knowing that Mrs. Waymon was there looking after us was always a personal comfort to me because I knew that she had the best interest of all of us at heart. The prison is now long gone and hundreds of new, expensive homes dot the landscape. A few buildings, one now an art gallery, are the only reminders of the not too distant past.

What I learned:

- Far more than learning to read and write takes place in a school.
- There is no substitute to feeling like you are special and that folks look out for you.
- Teachers in a school where there are many social and financial needs are a special breed, almost like modern day missionaries.
- Money still talks.
- There are exceptions to everything.
- A school and a reformatory do not go well side by side.

Sweet Pea and Baby Boo

In the mid 1970's the Commonwealth of Virginia required each school to develop a program for their gifted or advanced students. Our local school system urged us to think "out of the box." As we planned, it seems that we certainly did exactly that. The teacher who offered to work on this project with me was a creative, well-loved and respected teacher as well as an animal lover. As we were somewhat rural, we decided that we would focus on raising animals to give the students a totally different learning experience and help develop some responsibility. We settled on securing one or two goats and calling the program "Goats for the Gifted."

Somehow, we convinced the school system that this was a reasonable project, and we were allowed to convert the cinder block outdoor storage building on the side of the playground to a goat barn. We proceeded then to build a fence in an area of the property along the highway which was covered with poison ivy and little used as a result. Thus, the goats had ample room to run. The reformatory was always seeking ways to make themselves look better to the community. They operated a large and successful dairy and offered to deliver hay for the goats on a weekly basis and put it in the barn which they did.

Now, none of us knew anything at all about goats, including where to get one. We contacted our 4-H agent who put us in touch with a family who raised goats. The teacher, several parents and I, along with about 16 fourth, fifth and sixth grade students, went trekking off to the country on a Saturday and ended up with two goats, Sweet Pea and Baby Boo, which we bought for $75 each. We soon learned that Sweet Pea and Baby Boo were pure bred Alpine Dairy goats that would need to be milked twice daily as they got older. We also learned of an organization called the American Dairy Goat Association which together with 4-H offered ample materials and support either free or at a reasonable price. Thus began one of the most pleasant, happy and fun experiences of my career. Not only did we become familiar with the Dairy Goat Association but more importantly with 4-H which proved to offer wonderful educational opportunities for all of our students.

We were ready to be educated in goats! We could shut the goats safely up in the barn at night. It had steel doors which guaranteed they would be safe, but what would we do on weekends? They could not remain closed up for that length of time in a barn? One of our adventurous Goat Club families, the Stevens', who lived on five acres offered to keep the goats on weekends. Mother was a teacher in another school system and seemed to realize that there was benefit for the kids in what we were doing. They built a shelter on their heavily wooded property and constructed a fence so that the goats would be safe. My job, in shirt and tie, was to put the goats in the back of my nice Dodge station wagon and transport them to the Stevens' house after school on Friday. The Stevens' would return them on Monday morning. Usually Matt and Bonnie, the Stevens' kids, rode with me to keep the goats in the back and prevent them from jumping over to the seat. Goats are not easily potty trained and so we would put down plastic sheeting to cover the rear carpet. This was marginally successful. As the station wagon was our family's only vehicle, my wife was never particularly fond of this arrangement and it became my job to make certain that the back of the car was clean and free from goat odors.

The next problem was the twice a day milking. Who was going to milk them? We had been cautioned that as dairy goats they just could not be left 24 hours without milking. And who knew how to milk anything, not me!! Our first project was to build a stanchion to secure the goats while milking and for the students to take lessons from one of the dairymen at the reformatory as to how to milk. Learning was quite an experience with the "I think I've got its" to "I just can't make anything come out." I was a city boy, so learning to milk was an experience for all of us, students and adults. I am certain that had anyone been watching us, they would have found it a most amusing sight. As we learned milking, the students would offer "high fives" of congratulations to each other as the objective was mastered. We were all secretly pleased with ourselves that we were now country folk.

With the enthusiastic support of the parents, each family agreed to return to the school between eight and ten o'clock one night a month, Monday through Thursday, to milk. In the four years that I was connected with the Goat Club project I do not think we ever missed one night of milking so great was the commitment and interest of the students and parents. We had finally completed the basics.

The Goat Club met weekly after school. What would our agenda be? Always available, 4-H again rescued us. Through our local 4-H Extension Agent, Ann Matthews, who actively supported us, we not only learned about goats but 4-H also. 4-H offered a dairy goat project complete with text, workbook and materials and also offered such annual activities as Public Speaking, "Presentation Day," a talent show, and the culmination of all of our work, the County 4-H Fair.

We involved youngsters in all of these 4-H projects, the best of which was Presentation Day. After being taught the fundamentals of a good presentation, individual students went before judges and made well organized presentations from memory with visuals about something they had learned or were interested in. Our presentations were most always something to do with goats. The lessons learned as a result of Presentation Day included confidence, organization and the ability to successfully present oneself in front of a group. Indeed skills that lasted a lifetime.

The big event of the year was the 4-H Fair. The Goat Club got to show our goats. By the time we got to the fair, the students dressed in white show clothes, paraded the well-manicured, polished and dearly loved goats. Sweet Pea, who did not always behave herself, had learned to stand, pose and perform before a judge. We had learned that when a goat did not behave, bite her ear and it would calm her down. The poor goat had her ear bitten so many times it is a wonder she still had an ear, but it worked. The students were thrilled when we won a ribbon or a trophy, and they were recognized for their efforts.

Success having been achieved at our local fair, the students decided that they would like to show the goats at the State Fair in Richmond. Our first year was a real learning experience, and the goats showed well. Did you know that folks curl up with their animals in the barn stalls and sleep there? Thank goodness there were showers available because our kids did like the farm folks, met people attending the fair and told them about our school and our program.

Our second year showing at the State Fair was all about victory!! We won! Not only did we win all of the 4-H classes, we won all of the adult classes as well. To top it off, Sweet Pea won the "Best in Show." Students were given all kinds of accolades, ribbons, trophies and engraved silver. Boy, were they proud when they returned to school the following Monday with the famous Lorton School Goat. Some of the large breeders in the state were not too happy that an elementary school with two goats could win "Best in Show." The judge, a Presbyterian minister from rural Wisconsin, was firm with his selection and really seemed to appreciate the enthusiasm of the children.

With such an outstanding goat, the students wanted some baby goats, called "kids." We were not within several hours of any reputable breeders. Studying the monthly "Dairy Goat Journal" magazine, award winning studs were always advertised. We realized that we were not close to any of them. Someone came up with the idea of artificial insemination. Another chapter in our goat life was opened. We learned that we could order goat semen from across the country and have it shipped in a liquid nitrogen container which we would then return to the shipper. The reformatory dairy had a liquid nitrogen tank that they offered to let us use. After much study, the students decided to order semen from a grand champion stud in Arizona and have it shipped to us. My wife received a call at our home one day thereafter from the Greyhound bus station in Dumfries, Virginia, somewhat south of us. The station master advised that he had a tank of goat semen for Lorton Elementary School, and then added, "What kind of school is that anyway?"

We obtained a book on artificial insemination in animals, read it and decided to give it a try. One afternoon after school sixteen students, the teacher, an aide and I put Sweet Pea in her stanchion and completed the task following the step-by-step directions given in the book, one holding the goat, one holding the book and one holding the equipment. We watched carefully over the next several weeks to determine our success and behold Sweet Pea was pregnant. Not one soul ever said that was sex education or that it was inappropriate.

Five months later as a family was feeding one evening, Sweet Pea was about to deliver. A message quickly went out on the Goat Club telephone tree that Sweet Pea was having her baby, and the students and parents quickly gathered at the school. Sweet Pea delivered two beautiful baby kids as everyone watched and cheered. It ended up being a powerful learning experience for all of us, students and adults. One of our teachers, Marcia Tate, the wife of an Army General, was so taken with the babies that she insisted on keeping them at her home in the family room for the weekend. I often wondered what General Tate thought of the arrangement.

Showing goats, 4-H activities and watching the birth of babies was hardly the extent of Goat Club activity. We learned to pasteurize milk, make goat cheese and to cook all kinds of meals and desserts with goat milk. Next to animals, kids loved to eat, especially when they had input into what was being prepared. Our cheese was the worst attempt at cheese ever, and we didn't try again. On one occasion we were to make rum cake using goat milk. As was the usual practice, everyone was to supply an ingredient. Missy's job was to supply the rum flavoring. As we sat after school to begin, Missy went to her backpack and pulled out a fifth of rum. I figured all of us adults would be fired because alcohol in school was a definite "No! No!" Missy proceeded to very calmly tell us that there was no flavoring in the house so she just brought the rum. She knew her parents would not mind. She obviously did not get the connection between the real stuff and the flavoring or the connection that it should not have come on the school bus. We did not make rum cake that day.

Just recently I was contacted by a former Goat Club student, now 41 and a Navy Commander, stationed again in our metropolitan area. He reiterated that the Goat Club was one of the highlights of his school career and one he wished his own children could experience.

What I learned:

- Children do indeed have a natural love for animals.
- The study of goats taught us lots of valuable lessons that we did not expect to learn.
- The reformatory could indeed be an asset.
- "Hands-on learning" is fun, and the memories are great.

A Cast of Characters

Schools are like people. Each has its own uniqueness, its own set of values, and its own philosophy. Schools are built upon the people, the students and staff who inhabit them. Everyone brings their experiences with them when they come. Their stories, happy, sad, and funny are the flavoring that makes a school unique above the basic mission of teaching and learning. No one looks back upon their years in school and remembers the reading book they used or the history lesson they read and answered the questions that followed. People look back with fondness on the people and events that made their school lives special for them. They look back on the wonderful experiences that carried them through their lives: The trips, the activities, the fun. We all rejoice in the memories of school that we hold dear in our hearts and minds. Every day in school the foundations for life are laid. Everyday, teachers and staff have the opportunity to make life's foundation positive in the lives of all we teach.

The people we come in contact with daily shape us, children

and adults. Among them are always those real characters who stand out to each of us like a young, recent newlywed and well-loved fourth grade teacher, Mary Crocker, who brought her lunch to school every day in the finest china, a wedding gift I am certain and the only set of dishes the couple had. She never remembered to take any of the dishes home until they piled up in the classroom and there were none left at home. The kids would remind her to take her dishes regularly because they were concerned that she might not have any more dishes or that one might get broken and then what would she do? Or, Jennifer Pratt who thrived on creating lessons and games for her students and then would laminate everything so that it could be reused until the day that she got her suede tan blazer caught in the laminator with her in it. As the machine pulled closer to her and her jacket, we heard screams and ran quickly toward the lounge to find a totally panicked teacher hugging the laminator and it still running. We got the laminator stopped but had to cut part of her blazer off to get her out. She didn't laminate much after that.

I've already mentioned Mrs. Rhodes, our secretary, who was one of those characters. Once you got past her initial gruffness, you learned how much she loved our school and community. No one was going to criticize our school, our community or our staff for anything without recognizing her wrath. My relationship with Mrs. Rhodes had improved greatly since my arrival and since the installation of air conditioning in the office. Indeed, we had become quite good friends. One exciting day was the arrival of our first electric typewriter, an IBM Selectric. We were amazed that we could just pop those little balls in and out changing the font on anything easily. I am sure that we often changed the font on documents just because we knew we could do it to create variety. We were coming into the modern age. The state had developed an electronic system so that Mrs. Rhodes and I no longer had to spend the summer manually checking each teacher's "Virginia Teachers Register," their record of daily student attendance. This was required by the state, along with reasons for absence, and was directly related to the funding to school systems received. Of course each system wanted all of the funding they were entitled to.

One situation that Mrs. Rhodes did not handle well was the day that our very pregnant kindergarten teacher went into labor. In what seemed like a matter of moments, she delivered a baby girl on the couch in the office. When the paramedics arrived, it was Mrs. Rhodes, and not the mother, who most needed them. All in a day's work!

Classroom teachers have always been the heartbeat of every school. Among those countless teachers, Mrs. Janet Fox was special. Humor is a special quality and those who possess a good sense of humor often stand out to us. A sense of humor can turn the most routine activity into something exciting. The following are several notes to the office from Mrs. Fox, our local comedian:

"Sometimes my mom lets us cuss when we be good," quote for the day from Tony, a third grader.

"When will it ever end:
- Trevor had to give up three of his multicolored pencils to classmates because he broke theirs
- Christy lost her lunch money after bringing it in an envelope for the first time this year

- Matt is off his diet and yelling at everybody
- Jermaine came to school with no pencil again
- Joey wants to wear our special class shirt two days in a row instead of taking turns
- Jeremy is accusing Kimberly for taking his orange chair (all of our chairs are orange)
- Gwen fed our baby chicken water and gravel. It died.
- I had fun yesterday!!"

Mrs. Fox was equally a master at motivating students. She arrived early and wrote special individual notes to students on small slips of colored paper praising or encouraging them. Students taped the notes to the front of their desks to form long chains hoping they could get theirs to reach the floor. Those notes became their brag book, every student striving to get a note each day. There has never been a substitute for praise or commendation no matter how small. Mrs. Fox was also an artist. She engaged students in the simplest art lesson and then made certain that every single child was successful. Thus, they all became artists.

When Mrs. Fox retired, Michael Simpson wrote the following:

"I'm in Mrs. Fox's third grade class along with 23 other children, 4 birds, one guinea pig, one turtle, two fish and a rabbit. Our class mice died recently. All of us kids, birds, rabbits, guinea pigs, turtles and fish will miss Mrs. Fox very much. Mrs. Fox, like any other teacher, can be a big pain in the neck. If you don't pay attention, if you don't try as hard as you can, or if you don't do your homework--she goes nuts. I'm telling you that lady has scared my pants off more than once.

Mrs. Fox is a wonderful teacher. She taught us how to write, how to add and multiply big numbers, and how to spell plenty of words. She also taught us about nature. In fact, we spent many hours outside exploring plants, animals, the ground, the woods and stream near our school. Many days I'd come home from school with my pants and shoes full of mud. I don't think my mom ever really believed me that my teacher was responsible for all of this mess. But we loved going outdoors with Mrs. Fox and we really learned a lot.

My mom and dad have tried to explain to me what it means that Mrs. Fox is retiring. It's hard for a kid to really understand what retirement means because we've never had a job. I personally don't know why Mrs. Fox should stop teaching because she looks perfectly good to me, she doesn't act old and she doesn't look like a person who would be happy sitting in a rocking chair.

We love you Mrs. Fox and hope that you will remember us too, even when you're old."

Being a classroom teacher is not always as straight forward as it appears. You are daily in the position that you can be accused of anything by a student or parent, true or not. First grade Lorraine, pitiful and frail, had been beaten badly enough that her parents took her to the emergency medical clinic. The staff at the clinic immediately realized that the child had been beaten and made inquiries of the parents who adamantly exclaimed that Mrs. Saunders, the classroom teacher, had beaten the child when she had gotten into trouble in school. Mrs. Saunders, the mother of five with a long and glowing history at the school, was forced to contact a lawyer though we all knew that she had done nothing. The family went so far as to call each parent in the class and tell them that Mrs. Saunders had beaten their daughter and to watch for marks and bruises on their children. Indeed the parents were trying to make a case against the teacher and put her in a most uncomfortable position. With the support of the school system and the teachers association, we were able to show that Mrs. Saunders had done nothing to the child. The father finally admitted that he had beaten the child with an umbrella. In the end, Lorraine's mother killed the dad shortly after the resolution of the situation. Mrs. Saunders was left to rebuild her trust with the parents and community; Lorraine's family was left to rebuild their lives.

Another real character was Mrs. Cindy Creech, the art teacher. In a perpetual good mood, Mrs. Creech looked at the bright side of everything. She was a master at motivation but not the tidiest person. She saw that every student had weekly creative art opportunities. She used an assortment of media to provide these experiences. If you were throwing it away, Mrs. Creech was collecting and indeed using it. The art room as a result, looked like a junk pile most of the time. As her room was along the main hallway I always had Mrs. Creech keep her door closed as I did not want a school system official to walk down the hall and remark, "What's this?"

Our building was old, and the walls were empty. We had no tile on the walls, just bland light gray paint. Mrs. Creech decided that since we seemed to be the rest stop for travelers we would create a Virginia environment around us. Mrs. Creech designed an archway at the beginning of the hallway full of painted greenery and dogwood flowers, the Virginia state flower. Beyond that she had students paint the history of Virginia on our lower walls. She created a Presidents of Virginia section, famous Virginian section, products of Virginia section, geography of Virginia section, famous places in Virginia, etc. The older kids painted the walls proudly. Mrs. Creech sometimes touched up so that every student would be proud of their part. Thus, we created a meaningful history lesson for students and visitors around us every day, one that the kids would continually stop and study.

Mrs. Creech knew one of our parents, Mr. Tom Friar, was a famous wildlife artist. He received the Duck Stamp Award and often painted for the National Zoo. Contacting his wife, we received signed prints of his paintings which he signed, "To the children of Lorton School." Through the "Washington Post," Mrs. Creech was also aware that there was a prisoner at the reformatory whose art work was gaining prominence. A call to the reformatory and we were blessed with other original art work, thanks to him.

Notes from two students both of whom became teachers, one in our local community, reflect on the memory and the love for Ms. Creech:

"I really miss Mrs. Creech, as we always reminisce about our good times at Lorton. People were surprised at our stories about the goats, the camping trips, etc. It is different having one of your former teachers as one of your peers...."

"I am not sure why so many terrific memories have stuck with me, but I think it is because of the creativity of you, Mrs. Creech and all of my teachers. From letting us paint the walls, to the Goat Club, to really emphasizing the uniqueness of our school, all these things (to name a few) have influenced me and in turn, I want to do the same as a teacher."

Mrs. Creech could find the humor is every situation. The cap for the fuel oil tank was just outside of her classroom on the parking lot. As I was by her room one day and the oil tank was being filled, Mrs. Creech said to me, "Do we have a new oil tank? I have never seen them put the oil in there before." To my horror, the fuel oil was being offloaded in the septic tank instead of the oil tank. Though the maintenance department was not amused, Mrs. Creech and I thought it was the funniest thing and replied, "Only at Lorton."

Miss Johnson was a very serious teacher in the older part of our building. She expected that there would be "no funny business" in her class. Our floors in the oldest part of the building were wood that were sanded and varnished every summer. Indeed, when school opened, they sparkled. The floors, however, had small holes about two inches in diameter drilled in them so that termite and pest treatment could be added periodically. As the years progressed, the wooden plugs that were designed to fill the holes fell out and were often not replaced. One day Mrs. Creech came after me in a panic. Miss Johnson was in trouble, "Come quickly." I hurried to the room to find Miss Johnson on top of her desk, the kids screaming and out of control. A mouse had come up through the hole in the floor and was running about the room. Miss Johnson was terrified. We got the kids and the teacher out of the room and called maintenance as an "emergency" because we had mice coming up through the floor. Shortly thereafter one of the maintenance men arrived with a dozen mouse traps for us to set. Not the kind of repair we were expecting.

Counselors also played a critical role in the life of the school. Unfortunately because they did not have a regular class, they sometimes ended up with some not very pleasant duties:

"George-You cannot believe how the cafeteria went today. I was able to play the role of the custodian, hostess and server. Teachers still saw me as the Assistant Principal. I got to take care of eight discipline problems while handling the above. I shelled out $17.50 for lunches and battled with children who did not know what an egg roll was and then did not like it when they chose it. Some teachers picked their children up in thirty minutes, others forty or so. Rice and sweet and sour sauce flowed. The substitute custodian told me that the pan of water that the "clean up" towels stay in spilled and needed to be cleaned up and replaced. All of this plus dismissing and seating students. Plus one class ten minutes early to the cafeteria and one class seven minutes late. My lunch, taco salad, was cold and inedible. That was just lunch. I'll tell you the rest later." Years later at a promotion reception I asked what she had learned as counselor. Her first response, "To eat lunch standing up."

On another occasion: "Mr. T-Neil called Mr. King an asshole three times today. I suspended him from school until his mother and father come to school with him for a conference. She is going to set up a conference after the vacation is over."

Fifth grade Cara arrived just bawling and needing to speak to the counselor one morning. She was upset because her cat had died. When I asked how the cat died, she proceeded to tell me that the cat was asleep in the clothes dryer with the door open. Not knowing the cat was in there, mom had put clothes in the dryer and when they opened the dryer the cat was dead. It was funny to us but certainly not to Cara who spent part of the morning with the counselor until she was able to calm down and go to class. You never know what joys, problems or sadness students will bring to school on any given day.

The poor substitute:
To "Mrs. Kite (first grade teacher) I have the most respect in the world for you. I feel sorry for anyone who has to deal with this class day after day. What ever they are paying you can't be enough. Good luck with the rest of the year. Sincerely, Joe Peck. Kenneth was very bad all day long."

Until we got Mr. Roger, our wonderful Head Custodian, we had a terrible time with our custodial staff. The custodians were a set of characters all their own, not the funny kind. They didn't like each other, couldn't get along with each other, and were constantly afraid that one would do more work than the other. At one point in the evening we had two women, Mrs. Teresa Kemper and Mrs. Clara Walker. If one was off one day, you knew that the other would be off the next just so the work load would remain the same. One morning the following note appeared on my desk:

"Teresa, I have worked in this closet all night cleaning it up and its on your section. Thanks for your kind of cooperation. In the future all of your trash has to be removed every night. Clara."

Reply, "Clara, if its going to be kept clean we are all going to do it. It is not my responsibility alone. It wasn't clean when I came to work in here. I will be glad to cooperate in the future when there is fairness. All the trash is not mine. In case you don't see my note, as for the bucket in the cafeteria its not mine."

On another occasion two other custodians, Mrs. Wilma Cruise and Mr. William Batchelor were working at night. I got a call at home from Mrs. Cruise. "Mr. Towery, come quickly. I know Mr. Batchelor has been drinking and he is mad at me and if he gets to me he is going to hurt me. I've called the police on him." I proceeded to go to school as quickly as I could to find that Mrs. Cruise had Mr. Batchelor locked in a closet where he could not get out and she was right, he was angry. Thankfully, the police arrived shortly after I did and got them separated. I sent them both home. The school did not get a good cleaning that night. Mr. Batchelor never returned to work at Lorton.

From one of the custodians to Mrs. Simms, and Ms. Jones, teachers:

"I am so sorry I can't clean your room. Mr. Towery tore the vac cleaner all to pieces trying to fix it and it won't do anything now."

The individuals that made up the staff of Lorton as well as that of every school came in all shapes, sizes, and temperaments. We usually think of staff as teachers, however, each of the individuals that supported the teachers was just as critical to the mission of the school.

What I learned:

- It's not the building; it's the people.
- A sense of humor goes a long way in creating a positive environment.

- We all need to laugh at ourselves from time to time.
- As a teacher, you can be accused of anything by an angry parent or student.
- As teachers we routinely model for students who are having their values formed by what they see us do both good and bad.

Transitions

I thought Lorton Elementary School was the greatest place in the world. I loved the students, the staff and the community. Suburbia, however, was rapidly encroaching on our almost rural area, and we were becoming increasingly overcrowded. To relieve the overcrowding, the school system found it necessary to transfer about 175 of our students to several other schools. I knew that this would impact the complexion of our school with many excellent teachers and wonderful students leaving. Having completed ten years as principal of Lorton, which in our school system was a long time to remain as principal in one location, I thought it best to venture to another school. My boss had for several years asked about my willingness to go to Cameron School as principal. Cameron had a reputation within the system as a difficult school. So, with ten years under my belt, I decided to move on. Unbeknownst to me, Lorton had been my training ground for an amazing, often difficult, but always worthwhile, adventure that was to follow and carry me through the remainder of my career.

Cameron was indeed a very different school where I would spend the next thirty years. The building was modern, much newer and recently renovated. It sported a large gym, art and music rooms. Unlike rural Lorton, Cameron was one of the several schools in the system that one would consider urban. Most of our students came from small duplex housing and tiny single family homes that had been built in the late 1940's and early 1950's. Several large apartment complexes were also in our attendance area. We were close enough to the City that the new Washington area Metro transit system was about to open in the center of the community.

At the end of the preceding school year the School Board, after a long struggle, decided to close a number of schools where the enrollment had declined significantly. While the system overall was growing rapidly, older schools in the more highly populated, established areas were declining with partially empty buildings and small enrollments. Cameron had been one of those schools. Rather than closing it, a large number of students were being transferred in from several schools that were being closed. Our student population would be about 400 students with approximately half of the students African American and half Caucasian.

Having left a happy place, I arrived at Cameron to find the exact opposite. The existing students did not want the new students there. The existing teachers did not want the new teachers there. The new teachers had not wanted to leave their old schools, and they too were unhappy. Likewise, the community had not wanted their children transferred to other schools. One of the more affluent subdivisions did not want their children transferred to what was considered a "low income" school.

They petitioned the School Board to have their children transported to a more middle class community school by bus rather than have their children walk to our school. They won their fight.

As a result, Cameron was left to serve a largely low to moderate income school community. I discovered that I had new, unfamiliar challenges facing me as I had not worked in a racially diverse community. In addition, the moderate income population with whom I had previously worked was spread out over a large area rather than living in the close quarters in which these folks found themselves. As the residences were so small and by then current standards, inexpensive to purchase or to rent, there was a high turn over of students with families moving to an area with larger homes as soon as they felt that they could afford more. Most families rented their residences and did not expect to remain in them any longer than they had to.

When I arrived, I asked the PTA President if there were anything in particular that she would like for me to do. Her response was simply, "Like our kids." The first year was awful. I didn't know the students or the parents. There were lots of fights and bickering among both. Teachers were impatient, wanting everything taken care of and corrected in an instant in spite of the fact that the problems went far deeper than what was occurring at that moment. Some of the existing parents who had been active in the PTA wanted all of the problems solved but resented any attempts that I made to change the culture of the school. One group of parents decided that I was not welcome and sought to have me removed only to end up transferring their children to neighboring schools and then gradually bringing them back to Cameron one by one as things improved. With no Assistant Principal, I survived but barely, thanks to the overwhelming support of my superiors and the continued faith that they expressed in me. At the end of that first year many staff left for what they considered brighter opportunities elsewhere in the system, where there were far easier schools in which to work.

One of the greatest perks of the teaching profession is that you can annually put the past behind you and start fresh with the opening of every new school year. As I have never had a year that was as good as I thought it could have been, I have always appreciated that opportunity. The second year at Cameron was much different, even though many of the same problems remained. In addition to the support of two outstanding teachers who had come with me the first year from Lorton and a former "Teacher of the Year" who had transferred from one of the New England states, we were able to attract a number of real "Super Stars;" the finest the education profession had to offer.

Miss Sloane, a former nun joined our staff just out of the Catholic Schools in inner city Baltimore. She described herself as, "The only white person in an all black school", and was quick to say that she had skills in teaching reading that could help us. Mrs. Donna Dailey, a former library/media supervisor from Tucson, Arizona, whose husband had been transferred to the D.C. area, indicated that her skills too would be valuable to us. They joined a former Lorton teacher who had been transferred when the Lorton students and staff exited and a friend of hers who was likewise looking for a different school environment. Each of these individuals went on in their careers to become language arts and library supervisors, honored principals, or "Teachers of the Year." In addition, we were beginning to create a racially diverse staff which I considered essential in a school like Cameron.

Our academic task was monumental. Our overall reading test scores the first year were as low as the 27th percentile with math not much higher at the 39th. For the first time in my career I met students in grades five and six whom we called "nonreaders." In spite of having spent five or six years in school, they simply could not read. One of those students, a sixth grader, Preston, who had to put on a front as a really tough guy, spent hours in the office being tutored by all of us. He was totally lost in his classroom with the subject matter being taught well above him. I became determined he would learn to read so that he could at least feel academically comfortable with the kids in his class and not feel like an outcast getting into trouble daily, falling further behind, and being sent out of class. At the end of the year Preston gave me a book that he had written thanking all of us for the help that we had given him. Though Preston made a lot of progress, he still went on to middle school academically well below the ideal. Years later when I met him, I learned that he did indeed go on to finish high school, had a family and was working successfully in a construction job.

Teddy was one of our greatest academic challenges. A chubby and kind little boy, Teddy entered kindergarten as a blank slate. He did not know how to hold a pencil, a pair of scissors, had not used crayons and really had no idea what school was all about. Teddy had an outstanding kindergarten teacher, Mrs. Case, who did her best with Teddy but on the end of year first grade readiness test Teddy scored in the 5th percentile. We were saddened that all of our work with Teddy had resulted in such little progress. It was agreed that Teddy would spend a second year in kindergarten. Mrs. Case, with the support of the rest of the staff, redoubled efforts with Teddy to find that at the end of the second year in kindergarten Teddy scored only at the 15th percentile on the first grade readiness test. We would not give up, but could not keep Teddy in kindergarten. Everyone got involved working with Teddy and at the end of first grade he scored at the 39th percentile on the first grade test. By the end of sixth grade Teddy was certainly no scholar but he could read and pass a grade level test comfortably. At the end of that year Teddy and his family moved to a rural area of central Virginia and six years later I received a call from Teddy. "Would I please come to his high school graduation?" What an honor as I sat in the stands on the football field of Amherst County High School with his mother and his younger sister and watched Teddy walk across that stage and receive his diploma.

Another individual who joined our staff my second year at Cameron was Mrs. Sue Ann Daniels, our secretary. Transferring from another school and herself the mother of three, she was clearly committed to kids. Mrs. Daniels was a Girl Scout leader, a camper and a very motherly individual. As the secretary often sets the tone of the school because she is the first one folks see or hear, we critically needed one who was warm, welcoming and would present Cameron as the very best school around. Not only was she able to do that, she saw herself as critical to our mission and was able to use her skills to make our school happy, productive and efficient. We worked together for the next 29 years.

After a year, and with staff that was both excited and committed, it seemed we were on the way toward making a real difference for our kids.

What I learned:

- We all need some "Superstars" to aide us in our task.
- Kids who can't read, really can't read.
- You've never experienced it all in spite of what you often think.
- School hands you new challenges and new rewards every day.

"The Quality of the Future Starts Here"

As a child I was repeatedly told by my father, "Get your education. It is the one thing that no one can ever take from you." I heard those words, memorized those words, but never fully understood those words until I had been principal at Cameron for a while and had established a trust with the community. Parents would walk in off the street and ask us, the staff and me, to look at forms they had filled out to see if they had been done correctly. They asked us to make phone calls for them, to read something they had received in the mail and explain it to them, to write a note for them so that they could copy it and turn it in to whomever or even accompany them to an appointment so we could explain the situation to them. We filled out countless forms for Social Security, wrote numerous letters to immigration, explained taxes, contacted Family Services, verified living arrangements, etc. As such, it began to occur to me that knowledge is truly power. Those who do not have the knowledge are powerless. The ability to read, write and think is everything. I had never thought of myself as a particularly powerful person before, but I began to realize just how true my father's words had been. As I looked at our community, I realized the extent of what many thought I was able to do was as a result of my education and what truly needed to be done in and for the children of Cameron School.

At about that same time I came across the phrase somewhere that stated, "The Quality of the Future Starts Here." That seemed quite profound in terms of our students. Indeed, the quality of our future as a Nation begins in the classrooms of the elementary schools across this country. But, more specifically, the quality of the future of our children's lives at Cameron Elementary School would begin in our school building. If our children were not taught well and with urgency, many would end up in the same situation as that of their parents, having to take their important papers to someone else to interpret and explain. Education was the key out of the situation many found themselves in. I reasoned that Cameron School must do a better job of teaching than middle and upper class schools where the students were going to learn, go to college, have tutors, private lessons, etc. until they achieved and were academically successful. If the students at Cameron didn't learn at Cameron, scores of them would never again have the opportunity to learn. Thus, we adopted the motto, "The Quality of the Future Starts Here" not as just nice words, but as an understood reality that we, the staff, were responsible for ensuring a positive future for the children of our community.

The overwhelming majority of families in our community embraced education and embraced the school. We got terribly aggravated with others who seemed to ignore their children and still others who simply shortchanged theirs. While it could be a thankless task, 99% of the time educating our children was the most wonderful and important job one could ever do.

We were successful in creating happy kids who were good citizens and high achieving learners. Good teaching, love, compassion and caring were our greatest resources. Students and parents knew that they and their children were cared for, respected and appreciated. They returned that to us 100 fold by working in every possible way to meet our expectations. Midway through my career I discovered that a passion for teaching, love and caring were more powerful than anything else that takes place in a school. A passion for teaching most often resulted in student motivation, inspiration, encouragement and achievement. Those four elements, necessary for maximum learning, could take the most unfortunate children and make them believe that they were the most special children anywhere. Kids do not work for teachers and principals they don't like. Parents do not support schools that they believe really don't care about their child/ren. With these components in place, we were able to let children know that they were capable of doing anything. This was evident in our test results, in the pride in our community, and in the joy in our hearts when we knew one of our kids had succeeded even at the smallest thing.

I was thrilled when our annual summer recreation center opened last year to discover that the four recreation leaders were Cameron graduates. All soon to be juniors in respected colleges and universities, their majors included English, Nursing, Forensic Science and Psychology. They did an outstanding job running a large, well-attended rec center. These were not the "gifted" kids. These were our regular hard-working students committed to getting ahead through their educations. Each spoke of the struggles of their parents to "keep them straight," motivated and encouraged to move forward with their lives in positive directions exceeding the level of their parent's education. They were proud of themselves, and we were proud of them.

I received the following note from a former student several weeks ago. It reminded me again just how thankful I am that I do what I do and encouraged me to continue to do my very best every day for our kids. They deserve it:

"Dear Mr. Towery,
After so many years I find myself looking back recalling so many memories that I treasure in my heart. Cameron was my second home, my playground, my sanctuary. Cameron made me who I am today. I want to thank you for everything you did for me. From the fun field trips to busting me out of trouble, you have made me a better person today. I don't know how to put my thoughts into words right now for so many emotional memories are scattering through my mind. Mr. Towery, you deserve the world. You have always been my role model. Tomorrow I graduate from high school. I am going to be a doctor because I want to help people. Thank you for your time, advice and guidance. I will never forget you.

Rodney White"

The task has not always been easy for schools like ours. As a staff we realized that many of our youngsters daily had life experiences far different from ours. Many had done more and seen more by age 12 than most of us want to do or see in a lifetime. Mrs. Daniels, our secretary, said to me one day, "I've learned more about life and living in the five years I've been here than in the 50 years before that." We all learned so much.

Education on the streets was often a matter of survival and far different from that of a comfortable classroom. Students brought to school adult pressures that they lived with every day. As a child I lived in the same house until I was 12 years old. I knew that when school closed for the day I could go home and our family would still be living in that same house and that my parents would be there. I never doubted that. For some of our students, their lives were totally out of their control. Students went home to find that they had been evicted, that mom's new boyfriend had moved in or out, that dad had beaten mom and gone to jail, that they no longer had any hot water or electricity, that tomorrow would be there last day at Cameron because they were moving and they didn't know where, or that they would have to sleep in the car in the back parking lot tonight because there was no place else for them to go. These situations occurred every day.

As a staff we learned a lot about whose parent/s were drug dealers, what it was like if you had a parent in jail, what you do if you can't get along with your mom's boyfriend, etc. My heart broke for a fourth grader who went home to find that his family had been evicted only to come to school the next day to find that one of the kids in his class was wearing his clothes that had been taken from his front yard when all of their "stuff" was thrown out. Explain that one to a crying child.

Mrs. Daniels came to me at the end of one day and said that I was needed in the front office as there were two terrible looking men there to see me. Indeed, they had scraggly hair, leather jackets, multiple earrings, tattoo's, piercings, etc. They certainly were frightening looking people. I think she was afraid for all of us. In meeting with them I learned that they were undercover narcotics officers and they had set up a stakeout in the parking lot to arrest one of our student's fathers at dismissal because he was going to pick the children up from school. The arrest went off without a hitch except that two wonderful, smart little children were left at school not knowing what to do, what was happening or where to go. It must have been difficult to see one of your parents in hand cuffs. We were able to get the children home safely. Several weeks later, I received the following letter from J.C. a third grader, one of the children, who provided the address and asked that I send it to his dad:

"Dear dad. I miss you and did you get my letter. And I put my pictures in this letter for you too see and have. I love you! I love you! I love you." There was a heart drawn below. The letter was unsigned.

Following that, I received a letter in the US Mail from the father.

"Dear Mr. Towery,

I am writing you because I need your help. At this time I am in (Correctional Institution) for a drug problem. I hope to go back to Alexandria soon where I would ask for a reconsideration of my sentence and also try to get in a program at the Men's Home and I would be able to help my family. At this time my wife is having a very hard time with our bills.... I am asking you if you would write a letter to Judge____, telling him that I am really needed by my family if they are to keep up with the bills.

My lawyer said that your writing a letter to this effect would help me get into the Men's Home program. There I can work during the day and get treatment at night..............
Sincerely,"

I never heard from the father again. The children were in and out of Cameron a number of times. The situation in their family worsened as both mom and dad ended up in jail. One of our teachers, Mrs. Fox, took the children into her home and kept them for the last four months of the school year as there was nowhere for them to go and no one else able to keep them.

Life in the neighborhood was tough for some. Children were often scared simply by their surroundings and what they saw and heard every day. In school we offered a lot of reassurance, (call it counseling if you wish), but always a listening ear, the hope and encouragement that things would get better. A friend of mine, a principal in Nashville, TN, constantly reminded me that one of the most important things we do in our job is listen.

On another occasion, two police officers arrived one afternoon and asked for Eric Templeman, a twelve year old sixth grader, but asked to speak to me first. They informed me that his mother had been found dead of a drug overdose in the home and that a close family member was required to come to the house and identify the body before it could be moved. Eric was the only close family member. There was just he and mom, so the unpleasant task fell to him. They asked if I would stay while they told him of his mother's death and if I would accompany him to the home.

While Eric was sorrowful, he was very brave for a twelve year old. It was not an easy task for either of us. Eric did not return to school with me but remained with a neighbor who was a close friend. The task of planning a funeral fell on our staff as we reached in our pockets and collected money from anyone willing to donate. We secured a burial spot through social services in the "paupers" cemetery which I did not realize existed today. The casket was little more than a wooden box. The staff provided a flower arrangement for the casket, the minister of one of the staff members offered the eulogy, but Eric did see his mother buried with some degree of dignity. Eric went out of state following the funeral to live with some distant relative, and we never heard from him again.

Fifth grade Tonya was obviously shaken by a shooting in the neighborhood and wrote the following several weeks later in response to her teacher's essay assignment:

"The Man Who Got Shot"

"It was January 10, my dad, mom's friend, brother and me had a big party. My mom said, "Tonya and Jeremy, come take a bath". We went up and my dad's friend left around 6:30 pm. My dad went to take out the trash. Me and my brother were taking a bath then. As his friend got in his car a gun shot went off. My dad was outside at the time. My dad's friend was closing his car door. Sam (my dad's friend) ran in the house. My mom ran downstairs with my brother in a towel. I was in the bathtub and I was scared to death. I heard another gun shot.

I jumped out of the bathtub and put a towel around me. My dad ran inside and my mom said, "What happened?" He said, "The drug dealers are having a fight and Big Tony shot George in the hand and George shot Tony in the chest. My mom called the police got some blankets and went outside to put them over him. We waited inside for the police and the ambulance to come. I went downstairs to my room and put my gown and robe on. Then I went upstairs and said, "Sam come sit beside me". Outside it looked like a zoo with the police cars, the firemen and their trucks and the ambulance. There was even reporters in my neighborhood. They put Tony on a stretcher and rolled him in the ambulance but George was gone so they sent a helicopter to search for him. My mom made me go to bed.

The next day at 6 am on the news they said that Tony had died. I went to school and Mr. Towery said "everybody who rides bus 1087 come to the POD," so we went to the POD and sat down. He talked to us and told us that we would be alright. We went back to class and the day was finally over. I went home and the neighborhood seemed quiet. That night I told my mom, thank god Jeremy and I are safe."

At times the surroundings for some of our children offered little hope. We, the school, provided the nurturing for our youngsters to rise above the circumstance and succeed. Tonya went on to a successful high school career and is single and is currently working in the area.

While there were many sad stories there were so many success stories like a young lady, Christie, who arrived at Cameron as a fourth grader having repeated a grade in another school system. She literally begged me to promise her that if she worked really, really hard I would move her up a grade to the one she should have been in. She held true to her promise, gave school her very best effort consistently, excelled as an athlete in high school, became involved in track, broke a number of state records and earned a scholarship to Arizona State University. She became the number 1 runner in the women's 400 hurdles in the United States and went on to compete in the Olympics in 1992. Regardless of ones circumstances, education can take you above that and for Christie it did.

Jeremy's mother was found murdered shortly after he started kindergarten, impaled to a tree in a wooded area of the neighborhood. Boy-friend is currently serving a life sentence for murder. Jeremy went to the custody of elderly grandparents both in poor health and in an equally poor financial situation. Grandma died while Jeremy was in school at Cameron. Grandpa died while he was in high school. Jeremy had a difficult time in school and home life did not offer many rewards. As a young adult Jeremy was in and out of jail for short periods on a number of charges. As soon as Jeremy was released, he headed for Cameron and said to us, "You are my family, I don't have anything. Can you get me a few dollars for some food?" Indeed, I am sure we were like family as we had been one of the few places he had been nurtured and cared for. We felt happy knowing that we had touched his life in some positive way.

Each of these portraits reflects the kinds of difficulties that many of our students endured and the dreams of greatness that many were determined to achieve. Regardless of the circumstance, our students did grow, achieve, succeed, and become responsible citizens. It was always an honor to know that when they left, our handprints went with them and they carried positive memories of their experiences at school.

What I learned:

- Education is still the best gift life has to offer and it is free for the working.
- Education is the key out of poverty and can change a life.
- There is no substitute for love and caring in the educational process.
- Regardless of the circumstances from which they come, all children are special.

Oh! Those Parents

As a child your parents were your first teachers. Likewise, they were also your first role models and/or examples. Unfortunately as teachers we realized that too many parents failed to understand how much power and authority they had in dealing with their children as well as how much love and respect they had from their children. Others failed to realize that their children were learning from the daily messages their parents sent simply by what they said and what they did, both good and bad. If children experienced and felt love, they modeled it in return. If children knew that they were cared for, they became caring. If children knew that their education was important to their parents, education became important to the child. If a child watched as their parents helped them cheat on their homework, they learned that a little bit of cheating must be OK. As educators, we often became annoyed with parents who shortchanged their children for their own pleasures, desires or activities. As a parent myself, I felt our children were the most special gifts my wife and I had and our children grew up with that understanding. Unfortunately, for some of our Nation's children, that was and is not always true.

I casually asked a kindergarten child one morning last year why he was late for school. His response:

"Mama was in the bed with no clothes on and a man was in the bed with her with no clothes on and they couldn't get their clothes on in time for me to catch the bus. So, the man put his pants on and brought me to school. Can I still get breakfast?"

My first thought was, what else has he seen? As teachers we often had a lot to overcome as we tried to instill the quest and desire for learning. As children, they had a lot to overcome as they tried to put school and learning in perspective with the rest of the activities in their complicated lives.

The following note was handed me by the secretary:

"Keith Steven's mother, Mrs. Daily called. He is back with her here. She had gone back to North Carolina to "try again" with her boyfriend. She did not send him to school for a while because she didn't have any clothes for him because the boyfriend had them and wouldn't give them to her. So she and her mother went up and straightened it out. Now she has Keith's clothes and will send him to school on Monday. Only her or her mother is to pick up Keith, not the ex-boyfriend. He really hadn't missed too much school anyway because when he was out he was sick. Can he still get his lunch free?"

As teachers we consistently advocated for children because there were too few if any advocates for some. Kids don't make a salary and they don't vote, so often they were powerless to control any of their circumstances.

One of the issues faced periodically by our community was "babies raising babies." Too many children were raised by teen-age mothers with no training, preparation, money or prenatal care. One of our first graders was in the custody of his grand-mother because the mother was 16 and a minor. In at least two particular school years, we had sixth graders pregnant when school closed. One year there were three pregnancies. Though we never had a student give birth while still a student, they gave birth early in their seventh grade year, dropped out of school before graduation and relied on their families for support.

Though divorce and separation are not uncommon in our society, children do not always understand why this occurs. Sometimes they blame themselves for the fact that mom and dad are not together, even though it might be the best thing for the child. As they deal with separation, it can be made more difficult by the living arrangement agreed upon by the parents. There are many living arrangements today; some that seem to do little more than make it difficult for the child, especially in terms of education.

Several students lived with one parent one day and the other the next changing residences several times during the course of the week. When this was the case, homework, textbooks and supplies always ended up at the wrong house. Often children came to the office at the end of the day and asked where they were supposed to go today. Of course we most often didn't know. Or, how many times was a child returned to the school by a caring bus driver because they forgot where they were sup-posed to go until they got to the wrong place and no one was home? It would have been far easier if the child had remained in one house during the week and changed on the weekends.

At times we found cases where one sibling lived with the mother while the other or the others resided with the father, yet they came to the same school and saw each other every day. They wondered why they lived in different houses. Too often when a parent had difficulty dealing with behaviors, a child was passed to the other parent with the attitude, "I can't do anything with him (usually boys), here, you take him."

One of our greatest frustrations was the long absent father who for whatever reason decided to enter the picture and "ride in on the white horse" to save the child which usually ended in disaster because he had not been familiar with child rearing and often had seldom even been around the child. The same was true of "boyfriends". Mom developed a new relationship. The boyfriend moved in with a definite opinion of child rearing practices and decided he would "straighten out" the child. Soon the boyfriend was gone and the child simply left wondering. Many folks needed to realize that parenthood was a lifetime job and probably the most difficult job many of us will ever have.

James was a fifth grader. He was a good student who lived with his mother and step-dad, whom he called and knew as his dad. One day a well dressed gentleman entered the office and asked to see James because he was the father. James had never met or seen his father and did not know this man. However, the father had returned from court with the proper documentation, and we were told that we had to let the father see him. We sent a counselor with James but it was terribly unfortunate that this had to occur at school. After the father left and until the mother arrived, it was up to us to put the child back together. What a shame that mother and father had not been able to agree on a first meeting rather than having it end up at the school with only one parent and that one unknown to the child. Think how your life would have been impacted had a stranger entered your life one day and claimed to be the parent that you did not know you had. It would turn everything in your life upside down.

The school was often in the unfortunate position of refereeing disputes between parents, and we often received calls, usually from the mother, telling us that dad might come to the school to see or try to take the child. This put the school in very uncomfortable territory. We were forced to respond to the call that, if the parent who came could prove that he/she was the natural parent; we were required by law to let them see the child unless there was a court document that specifically stated otherwise. Such documentation almost never existed. Further, far too seldom or far too late was the school given copies of court orders that limited the right of a parent to visit, speak to or have access to a child.

The secretary came to get me in the cafeteria at lunch time one day and told me that I needed to come to the office. We had a really "strange" situation with a lady trying to register her two children. I went and found a youngish lady with a little girl, 8 or 9 years old and a little boy, 6 or 7. I asked them if they were coming to our school, and they nodded their heads as they were. I asked the little girl what her name was and she said Cinderella. I was not prepared for that and did everything in my power to keep from laughing. I told the mother that I did not think we should call her Cinderella in school as I was afraid the other children would make fun of her. I suggested that we call her Cindy. Mother and the child agreed. I proceeded to ask the little boy what his name was and he said Vine. I said the same to the mother and suggested that we call him Vinny. They readily agreed. As we began the registration process it became quickly evident that this would be no ordinary registration. There was no paperwork. There were no birth certificates or shot records. Mother explained that she was a palm reader. They lived in the small house on a busy corner of our community that had a large sign in the front yard that read, "Palm Reader, Tarot Cards." The children had been born at home, thus, there was never a birth certificate. The only record of birth was the date that the mother said they were born. The children had never had a shot, thus there was no immunization record. The children had never been to school and could neither read nor write. Mother said that they were a family of gypsies and that she had been only to the fifth grade herself. The dad, Dutch, was up north trading cars, and he did not want the children to come to school. The mother decided while he was gone it was time for the children to go to school and she wanted to make certain that they were in school before he arrived home. She knew if they were in school when he came home and they were happy that he would let them stay. But, if they were not yet in school, he would not let them begin. We worked with the school system and the Health Department. Mother agreed that she would take them and begin the process of immunization. Cindy and Vinny entered school happily and were thrilled with every new day which to them was just bursting with excitement.

I found it almost unbelievable to think that these children had been born in the 1990's in a suburb of the capital city of the greatest nation in the world. From their front door, they could see the George Washington Masonic Temple, a famous local landmark, yet they had never been given the opportunity to go to school or learn to read or write. I couldn't help but wonder if there were others out there with similar circumstance.

We always worked closely with parents to resolve their concerns. One memorable day, however, Mrs. Hicks and her husband came in, and she was angry. Of course, we had no idea that she was coming nor did we have any idea why she was angry. It seemed she thought someone was picking on her not so little Charlie. She barged through my office door and immediately began to scream at me using every possible foul word and statement she could muster. And it continued, very loudly!! The secretary quickly closed my office door and proceeded to block off the hallway outside of my office as the mother was so loud and verbally abusive she did not want the children to hear what was being said. There was no opportunity to address any of the mother's concerns because all she wanted to do was to vent, and on me. Finally, she ran out of steam, opened the door and left in the same manner in which she had come followed by her husband who had never said a single word. A few minutes later, her husband came back to my door, stuck his head in and said, "Don't pay a damn bit of attention to her." That was the last we ever heard from Mrs. Hicks.

On another occasion while I was in conversation with an elderly grandmother, my office door flew open and in walked a father followed by his wife. He commanded me to, "Stand up, I'm going to break your God damn neck." Mother was behind him holding an infant and saying to the father, "Don't hit him, don't hit him!" I was not struck but to say I was not somewhat frightened would not be truthful. Again, he believed that another child was picking on his child. Our children are special and should be our most loved possessions but, like it or not, we in schools do not have control over what people do or say. We can only teach respect for each other and address the problem once it has occurred. Don't we wish every day that we had answers to all of the problems?

What I learned:

- **Parents come in all shapes, sizes, temperaments and educational levels.**
- **Living arrangements are often confusing to children and even more confusing to schools.**
- **In a few short years, many children see and experience more than they should in a lifetime.**

Little Things

Whether it was the shiny floors in the lobby, the attractiveness of the bulletin boards, the remarkable student displays, the fresh flowers on the table, the clean aquarium in the hallway, or the smile when you entered the office, little things in our school made a BIG difference. One of these was the morning Grandparent greeters. Grandma Kathy was at the front door every morning to greet the children and Grandpa Tom at the back door to greet the school busses.

While this seemed like such a small thing, we soon learned that parents loved to see a smiling and familiar face when they pulled up to drop their children off in the morning. It gave them a sense of order and safety. Carmella was ready for a smile and warm hug from Grandma as she entered the building, so was Jose. Many of the children were coming with their little morning problems or from just having been fussed at by mom because they were running late. Staff liked the warm greeting they received as they began their school day with its complexities like the car that would not start, or the terrible Washington

D.C. traffic they had encountered in their effort just to get to school. Parents liked a smile and often a hug, especially those who had come to see a teacher because of a problem with their children.

Grandma and Grandpa had no written duties, no deadlines, no reports to complete. Their only job was to smile, wave, offer a hug, greet folks and just be there. They made such an impression in the neighborhood that one of our Grandma Greeters was featured on the local NBC television station recognized as the TV station's "Person of the Day". When, for whatever reason, Grandma and Grandpa were not there, people always asked about them. They started our day off in a happy and pleasant way.

We cheered for our grandparents daily! In these times, I do not know what we in the schools would have done without them. Countless children in our school and across the country were being raised by grandparents every day because, for whatever reason, parents were unable to care for them. They consistently, often without warning, stepped up to the plate and took over the raising of multiple grandchildren in whatever way they could, usually being wonderful parents on their second go round. One Cameron grandmother unexpectedly was called to travel to Texas to take custody of three of her grandchildren found alone in a hotel room. The whereabouts of the mother was unknown. This was not to be temporary, and she raised them to be responsible adults. That story was repeated over and over every day.

The Friday before Mother's Day was always Grandparent's Day. Organized by our grandparent greeters; grandparents and great grandparents were invited to accompany their grandchildren to school. Grandparents arrived from all over proudly escorted by their broadly smiling grandchildren. Many grandparents, especially those with physical issues, went to a great deal of trouble just to get to the school and get around once there. Others had travelled a great distance. Grandparents were greeted warmly by the Girl Power and Boys Leadership sixth graders and served a continental breakfast. They were invited to attend a program by our choirs and band where the oldest, those with the most grandchildren, often numbering in the teens, and those having traveled the farthest distance were always recognized with a carnation. Following, as guests, they visited the classrooms of their grandchildren where many spent the remainder of the school day and became instant celebrities sharing their own lives with the students. Having grown up in all corners of the world, it became a unique learning experience for the class. They loved to eat lunch in the cafeteria and appreciated the opportunity to visit. Most of all they loved to be with their grandchildren. For us it was a wonderful opportunity to spread good news about our school.

Our first priority in school was always the safety of the children. Unfortunately, that was not always the first priority of the parents. While most parents were considerate and kind, that was not 100% the case. My job, along with one of the teachers and instructional assistants, was loading the long line of cars as parents picked up their children at the end of the school day. The assistant principal and counselor loaded the busses at the rear of the building. The only satisfactory survival technique we found was to act like police officers. In spite of our efforts to organize parents in such a way as to enter the school driveway safely along narrow streets, many refused to cooperate until

Mrs. Stiles, one of our instructional assistants, daily stood at the corner and simply refused to allow cars to come in from the wrong direction. People didn't always like it but were forced to cooperate. Poor Ms. Timmons' duty was to cross the children in front of the school. She had to be on her toes to keep them and herself safe.

During the course of the school year we were often cussed at and fussed at for trying to get the children out of school and on their way home safely. One mother loaded her three children and several of her neighbor's children into her van. The children were jumping everywhere. I asked if she was going to put them in seat belts at which time she shouted obscenities at me, gave me the "finger" and drove away. Parents had one goal and one goal only in picking up their children at the end of the day. That was, "get them quickly." Many times we reminded parents to let their children get all the way in the car before they started off. One mother was in such a hurry that she ran over her son's foot as he tried to get in the vehicle.

Thomas was a gutsy patrol beginning in fourth grade. With his allowance, he proudly bought all of us, including him, bright orange vests and caps that said "Police." With his patrol belt, vest and cap, he stood out front at dismissal with a large pad and daily took down tag numbers of those parents who refused to cooperate or were driving unsafely. It was quite obvious what he was doing. He never hesitated to tell a parent that they were wrong and they knew he was right. Were you ever told off by a fourth grader knowing that he was right and you were wrong? I was amazed at his "gutsiness" but it worked, and he really helped us and his fellow students.

As the cars waited to pick up their children, one car load at a time, the parents would often blow horns and shout at each other. One father got out and threatened the father in the car in front of him because he would not move up quickly enough. We called the police as a result for fear that they were going to come to blows. As the day's duty ended, we were always refreshed and glad that no one was hurt, except at times some bruised feelings. We reentered the building with a daily collection of stories and laughs.

What I learned:

- Grandparents are among the world's greatest gifts.
- Grandchildren are as proud of their grandparents as their grandparents are of them.
- Student safety is not the priority of everyone.
- A gutsy patrol can make a real difference.

"Character Counts at Cameron"

"Character Counts At Cameron," as indeed it does at schools across the country. While we wanted our children to be successful academically, we also wanted them to grow to become good citizens who were both caring and productive. One of the spin-offs of our Alternative Education Program was the introduction of school uniforms. When we realized that the white shirts and ties of the Alternative Education students were having a positive impact on their academics as well as their behavior, others on the staff and in the community began to take notice. School uniforms at Cameron thus evolved.

At Cameron, uniforms were made up of red or white polo shirts or white blouses and navy blue pants, skirts or shorts. The most obvious element of our uniform was the red "Character Counts at Cameron" tee shirt which each student received without charge every school year. Through the neighborhood, the red shirt with large white letters was common. On field trips they helped us identify the students quickly and keep track of them more easily. They also improved safety in the neighborhood as Cameron students were easily recognized.

Parents repeatedly stepped forward to assist children in "Character Counts" shirts when there was a need such as helping second grade Gretel who missed the bus and decided to walk to school as no one was home. Mrs. Vasquez picked up Sonja and Angelina, grades 2 and 4, trying to cross a major intersection at rush hour. The parents had gone to work and the girls routinely got themselves off to school. They did not know what else to do, so they decided to walk. Parents also assisted with injured students in the neighborhood after hours or on the playground, when students fell and got hurt while playing. Still there were those little ones that simply got lost like kindergarten Joel, who thought he knew exactly how to get home by himself after school but didn't. Instead, he just roamed the neighborhood until someone found him. Unlike when we were children, many times when students were in need of a ride home I asked their address only to be told, "I don't know but I can show you how to get there."

Many students dressed in their Character Counts shirts every day, accumulated several through the years and passed them on to younger siblings. They were also for sale in the school store at a modest price. I was told by the staff at the local middle school that they saw them daily, worn proudly by former Cameron students.

Though I have no solid research that says school uniforms made a difference in student attitude and behavior, there is not a staff member at Cameron who would not tell you that they did. As a staff and as a school we spoke regularly with students about their learning attire comparing it to sports uniforms that were worn to their various soccer and football games. Simply, we all dressed in certain ways for certain occasions.

Cameron parents supported our school uniforms as they saved a considerable amount of money in a household that had little extra. Uniforms made it easy to dress their children and get them off to school in the morning. Parents, especially those from other countries and cultures, were used to uniforms in their own backgrounds, many having worn them to school themselves.

I asked our student government president, a sixth grader, if she would wear a uniform to middle school. Her response was, "Sure, if everyone else did." I think that was true of many of our students. Our students would tell you that in the uniform they were all alike. There was not a requirement to dress in a certain brand to be accepted into the group or to be popular. There was no pressure at Cameron with regard to clothes thanks to uniforms. One of the phrases that I heard repeated numerous times by our students was, "There are no snobs at Cameron." Uniforms were one of the reasons students felt that way.

Boys Leadership and Girl Power were two after school activities that promoted good character. Sixth grade students chose to participate in these worthwhile activities both designed to promote leadership, build self-esteem, and prepare youngsters for the future. In the two programs we talked about how to present yourself positively, how to plan and set goals for the future, who to hang around with and who to avoid. We talked about finances and what you needed to do to get a job and to gain the respect of others. We talked about role models, both good and bad, especially with regard to sports stars who many aspired to emulate. Both groups experienced dinner at a nice restaurant, a new opportunity.

With the boys we talked about leadership and qualities like honor, courage and commitment and gave them opportunities to respond. Our boys came from El Salvador and Honduras, from Ethiopia and as close as Alexandria. It was a global group of fine young men. They responded from their experiences and problems, sharing their devotion to and respect for their families. Some shared what it was like growing up and never having met or known a dad. Others talked about their individual struggles just getting to the United States and those family members who died as a result of that struggle. They talked about the number of foster homes they had been in and out of and what it was like to go to bed when you had no one to tell, "I love you." Still others spoke of what it was like when dad was in jail and they were afraid that he was going to be returned to the home country. They spoke of family handicaps and the impact that physical disabilities created in trying to secure a good paying job. They talked. They laughed. They cried. They shared. They routinely demonstrated incredible insight, courage and compassion which always left us proud of them and feeling hopeful for the future.

Many of our boys were from other cultures. Others came from homes where there was not a lot of money. They spoke, often tearfully, of their mothers' single handedly raising several children on a minimal salary. They were adamant in their desire to make their parents proud of them, as they knew their parents came to this country and worked in meager jobs for one reason only, so they, their children, could have a better life. The boys laughed when their friends laughed, cried when their friends cried and hugged one another out of compassion and understanding. Elijah said on one occasion, "It's our job to lift each other up." Indeed, they did exactly that and sought to understand each others burdens. They were examples of the way we all should live and made us want to be examples for them.

In Girl Power the initial talk was how to behave "like a lady" and act respectfully such that teachers and adults see your best side. They visited businesses, talked to those in charge and got a first-hand view as to what it took to get the job done. Girl Power also addressed "girl topics" like "make up" etc., clothes selection, careers and opportunities that heretofore have not existed for women. Our goal was that our students would aspire to work toward the careers of their dreams. Toward that end, we annually presented a Saturday GEMS (Girls Engaged in Math and Science)/Boys Leadership Conference with guest speakers who were leaders in science and math in respected organizations. Lockheed Martin and other area firms shared their best professionals with us to promote education, to encourage and to inform.

In Boys Leadership, the boys stood before their peers and spoke on various subjects weekly. At the beginning of the year they were very fearful and at the end, they all sought to go first. Their speeches went from seconds to minutes, from repeating what the first one to speak said, to creativity, individuality and deep thought. Two years ago the boys were asked to address a large group of school principals on leadership. Their comments were amazing. The boys left proud of themselves and we were equally proud of them. Boys entered Boys Leadership as students and left as leaders; models for the younger students crediting the program for their success.

One of the earmarks of Boys Leadership and Girl Power was to dress up on Wednesdays. The boys were anxious to don their shirts, ties and suits, "dressing for success," as it set them apart from the other students in the most positive way. As the year opened, we did not tell them to dress up, they simply looked forward to it, did it on their own and appeared "dressed up" at the first meeting. When guests visited the school, ie: School Board members, school officials, etc. or on Grandparents Day, Boys Leadership and Girl Power proudly served as hosts and hostesses.

What I learned:

- **Uniforms eliminate a lot of pressure on kids.**
- **Students, both boys and girls, jump at leadership opportunities.**
- **Students from other cultures speak freely and with great pride about their families and their desire to make them proud.**
- **While kids can be cruel, they can also be incredibly kind and "Lift each other up."**

"You Don't Know What They Do to Me, Mr. Towery"

One of the tragedies of modern society and the most difficult for me to deal with emotionally was the abuse of children: Mental, physical and sexual. On more than one occasion I had children, usually boys, drop to their knees in my office and literally beg me please, please not to call a parent the result of some sort of misbehavior. Their comments were, "You won't see me again for several days, Mr. Towery", "I will get beaten", or "You don't know what they do to me, Mr. Towery." Never did one say, "I will get a spanking", it was always I will get "beaten" or "hit." While a healthy fear of a parent's ire is often good, sheer terror is not and led me to conclude that the punishment given was often overdone. I was told by children that they were refused food, locked in their rooms, made to sleep out of doors and tied to the bed while they were being hit. Abuses were not just physical. The level of responsibility that was expected of some youngsters was often extreme for their age. One fourth grader moved so many times during one year that the mother attempted to keep him in our school by sending him on the Metro, bus and train, by himself from across the county with directions that when he got off the train, he was to walk to the school, about a half mile away. The mother of a second grade girl couldn't deal with her daughter any longer so she just gave her away signing over custody to a lady she really did not even know. Still another second grade boy, when mother was arrested, ended up in a group home because no other family member would even consider taking custody of him. He was in no way a problem child.

In some cultures punishments that we didn't consider acceptable were common with our children. Saeed was beaten with a shoe until his nose was broken and then refused treatment from a doctor and as a result must live with an obviously broken nose the rest of his life such that every time he looks into a mirror he is reminded of his misdeed as a child. First grade Jeremy made his father so angry that the father broke his leg and the child spent the next month or so on crutches, a constant reminder of his past actions.

Fourth grade Robert came into my office early one morning and told me that step dad had beaten his sixth grade brother Jimmy so badly that he had run away and spent the night out in the woods, "Could we go and get him?" We got in my car. Robert knew exactly where Jimmy was. When we found Jimmy, it was obvious that he had been brutally beaten with strap marks all over his body including his arms, head and face. Jimmy told me that step dad had wanted to beat him so badly that he had broken the door down in order to get to him. I said, "You mean the door has to be repaired?" Jimmy replied, "No, the door has to be replaced." I asked how he had gotten away from step dad and he indicated that he had jumped out of the second floor window and hid in the woods all night so that no one could come and find him. As the younger brother knew exactly where to find him, I suspect that he had hidden there before. Child Protective Services was immediately called, and the children did not return home. Several days later one of the children's neighbors, whom I did not know, came in to see me. He thanked the school for taking care of the situation and told me how ashamed of himself he was because he had known that such abuse was taking place in Robert's and Jimmy's home and had never made any attempt to do anything about it.

Physical abuse was only one small part of the picture, the part as educators we saw because there were physical signs. Not infrequently I had a parent scream at a child in front of me, "I hate you," "I don't ever want to see your face again," "You are the cause of all my problems," "If it weren't for you my life would be OK." We humans are very fragile, especially children, who just accepted the blame for all of the negative issues in the household. As a child, I grew up with the saying, "Sticks and stones will break your bones, but names will never hurt you". As an adult, I realized that most of the time words were far more painful than bruises. Bruises went away but "I never want to see your face again" said in anger does not; especially when it came from one that society dictates was supposed to love you.

Teddy said to me quite casually one day, "Jamie (first grade sister) wets the bed every night and dad makes her lay in it and won't let her change her sheets or put dry clothes on, Is that right, Mr. Towery?" Children have an inherent sense of right and wrong.

Debbie came to us as a fourth grader having been in a string of foster homes. As with most foster children, she held to the dream that one day soon she would be back with her parents. One day shortly after her arrival the social worker picked her up early. Many foster children did not trust their social workers because they regarded them as the one who took them away from their parents. On this particular day Debbie did not want to go with the social worker. As they exited the school, Debbie climbed to the very top of a tree in front of the school. After what seemed like forever, the exasperated social worker was unable to coax her down. As school closed for the day one of the teachers went out and he too was unsuccessful in coaxing her down. Finally it was my turn to try to get Debbie out of the tree. The social worker was long gone and it was getting toward dark. Debbie finally decided it was time to come down. At that point she realized that she was so far up in the tree that she was afraid to even move. I was not about to climb the tree. With the help of the custodian and secretary we were able to talk Debbie down in tiny steps saying, "Put your foot here, now here. Hold tight." Debbie finally came out of the tree and went to her foster home. Several years later Debbie was still in the same loving and caring foster home and in the same school. Her foster family supported her as had some wonderfully caring teachers. Debbie's grades and academic skills consistently improved and she was being successful in school.

I don't know what took place in Tommy's house but Tommy was a very bright but squirrelly little third grader always seeking attention. A few minutes before dismissal one Friday afternoon Tommy's mother came into the office with a suitcase and announced, "These are Tommy's clothes, I don't care what you do with him but I don't want him anymore." She quickly left. A call to Protective Services revealed that they were not at all anxious to take a case late on a Friday, "Was there anything we could do until Monday morning?" I called my wife and told her that we were having a house guest over the weekend. Tommy got along with my three children and went to Protective Service custody on Monday morning.

As principal, almost every year there was a child who begged me to take them home and let them live with my family. Such was the case with third grade Eddie. Father was in jail so he was sent to live with his drug addicted mother in Tennessee where the situation was even worse. He later related that he often found himself without food or a place to live and remembered going through trash looking for something to eat. Eddie was returned to Virginia to live with his grandmother and a severely retarded aunt. Every day he would beg to come home with me. Finally, I agreed to let him visit on a Saturday. I picked him up and my children and Eddie quickly became fast friends. Following that first visit, Eddie visited many Saturdays. When it was time for him to go home on Saturday evening, however, he would cry to the point that it became very emotional for our family. My wife finally told him that he had to quit pleading when it was time to go home or he would have to stop coming. He finally understood. Eddie faced many obstacles after elementary school, was in and out of trouble with the law but grew to become a productive, hardworking citizen with whom I am still in close contact. The caring some children experienced at and through the school was far more evident and encouraging than what they received at home.

LaToya was a bright and loving second grader who carried a body odor that grew increasingly worse to the point that the teachers and her classmates complained. The counselor, Mrs. Johnson, met with LaToya and fearing that there might be no hot water or shampoo at home invited her to take a shower at school in the clinic shower. She provided new clothes, underwear, soap and shampoo. When LaToya came out of the shower in her new clothes she was spic and span. Mrs. Johnson fixed her hair and LaToya went back to class very proud of herself. Mrs. Johnson went to clean up the bathroom and shower and discovered that LaToya's underpants were all covered with dried blood. A visit from Child Protective Services followed by a medical examination revealed that seven year old LaToya suffered from gonorrhea the result of severe sexual abuse. Sadly, many of our children, especially where multiple individuals share housing, a room or a bed experienced sexual abuse that was often unreported until months, even years, after it had occurred.

Many extended families shared residences to the point that became common in our community. I always worried when a child told us that they lived in a house on a particular street and then went on to say that mom, dad, brother, sister and baby had one room, the old people lived in the other room, and the men lived downstairs. They didn't know the names of any of these people who were not related to them. I was advised by the manager of an apartment building to visit an apartment where there was a "bunch" of children who were not going to school. I went and found thirteen people living in the apartment with only mattresses on the floor. We enrolled five of the children. Those were invitations for sexual abuse.

The counselor conducted classes with older students on "good and bad touches" annually. Frequently children, most often girls, approached the counselor following classes that resulted in identifying a number of sexual abuse cases. Susie seemed like a normal, happy and very bright sixth grader. She approached the counselor following the class indicating that her mother's boy friend was abusing her. Unfortunately, the mother emphatically supported the boy friend who denied the allegations. The child was called a liar, told she had made the story up, etc. The abuser was usually an "uncle", boy friend, step dad or one living in the home. All too often, the child was given the blame in these situations. In turn they had to go back into the home, with the guilt of having told, having created problems for the family and with the threat of being shamed for what they had said. Not only did we deal with cases of girls being abused by fathers, step dads or boyfriends, we saw boys abused in the same way, sometimes by their mothers. Our hearts broke for these children, and we could only refer the cases to Child Protective Services, offer encouragement and support telling them that they had done the right thing by reporting the abuse.

Perhaps the greatest tragedy that we ever encountered as a school community was the death of two sixth grade boys, best friends, struck by a car on New Years Eve. The driver was charged with driving while intoxicated. The students, especially those in sixth grade, were affected as many had never been close to death before and returned for the New Year to find two of their well loved classmates gone, their desks empty. While all of the staff felt the terrible loss, the role of the counselors was critical in working with the students to understand and move beyond the tragedy.

With a staff that did not change greatly from one school year to the next, the school became a very tight knit community.

When something happened to one child, everyone in the school and community was impacted by it. Death, injury, divorce, financial hardship, it all came through the school. While our first job was teaching; the love and caring relationships formed extended well beyond the classroom and the school building. This was not only true of current students but of former students and families as well. I often realized that as the school principal I was in the unique position of seeing a total community while most residents saw only their immediate surroundings. I valued and deeply treasured that part of my role as many lifelong friendships were formed. I sat in hospitals with the parents of seriously ill children, delivered food to families at times of the death of loved ones, and worked to see that families in trouble had the immediate resources they needed. I was invited to birthday parties, graduations, family celebrations and yes, even funerals, the result of being touched by our children.

What I learned:

- **Classes on good touches and bad touches help identify abuse.**
- **Some children see sexual abuse as the way life is.**
- **Unkind words said in anger or frustration can hurt as much as or more than a "beating" by a belt.**
- **Abuse is not limited to families of a certain income.**

Alternative Education

During my last 19 years as principal our school housed two elementary Alternative Education classes. If a child's behavior was such that they could not remain in their base school for any reason or if they had a history of severe misbehavior, they were sent to Alternative Education. These were smaller classes that not only addressed behavior but academics as well. Through the years we earned a reputation for handling challenging children well. Although most were indeed a challenge, they often became some of our most special kids.

The two Alternative Education teachers, Mrs. Carol Barnes, primary, and Dr. Laura Reynolds, upper grades, were master teachers and learned to handle almost any situation or confrontation. A visit to either class on any day revealed hard working, polite boys. Though we occasionally had girls, most always the class was made up of just boys. Never would one suspect that these were children who had been recommended for expulsion or had a history of severe, unacceptable behavior. Some of the children had an ongoing history of poor behavior; others had made a single mistake like taking a knife or other weapon to school.

When the program began, we had only one class with Dr. Reynolds, the teacher, and Mrs. Barnes, the assistant. As the need for such classes grew, Mrs. Barnes joined the teaching team as the primary level teacher. I remember well looking at the student records of the first class with Dr. Reynolds. We were shocked that they contained discipline report after discipline report that included everything from assaults on other students and teachers to bringing weapons to school. Our first thought became, "We don't know if we can help these kids or not." We concluded, however, that we could make them look nice. Thus, the program began with five or six young men wearing white shirts and ties to school every day. Though the boys were not happy with the arrangement, that soon changed as everyone began to compliment them on their appearance. We suspected that some had never been complimented on anything. Donated white shirts and ties began to change the lives of the boys who found they liked receiving compliments. Lest this sound simple, the challenge was just beginning.

Most of these children were severely deficient academically. They were almost all male, most likely poor, black, and lacked any form of social skills or the ability to get along with anyone. Each was out for himself or herself. As Dr. Reynolds would frequently remind us, they had spent so many of their school days in trouble, suspended or in the principal's office that they had indeed missed their education. They had survived by intimidating others.

Fifth grade Edwood arrived not being able to write or spell

his name (Perhaps mother couldn't either.) Few had any basis in math and at the beginning we didn't work directly on science or social studies because the needs in math and language arts were so great. Through the history of the program the first lesson of the morning was social skills; (taking turns, raising hands, kindness, perseverance, courage etc.,) words and ideas with which these boys were totally unfamiliar. We also celebrated any and every occasion.

Birthdays were special days with almost every child telling us that they had never had a birthday cake or a birthday party. These traditions continue today. Youngsters began to feel that they could be like the other kids, accepted and successful. They liked to eat, and they liked knowing that they were cared for even if they did have to wear a shirt and tie, eat breakfast and lunch with the teacher and seldom, if it all, have recess with the other children. They knew Dr. Reynolds loved them even if they misbehaved. As they worked, she constantly reminded them that one day of appropriate behavior was not sufficient. They had to behave and do it "consistently."

As students became more familiar with the program, they would step up and defend Dr. Reynolds when another misbehaved. They always told others new to the program as they enrolled, "Dr. Reynolds, she don't play!" They also learned as they met new students to stand, extend their hand, and introduce themselves appropriately. "Thank you," "please," "yes sir," yes mam," quickly became routine.

One of our favorite students we affectionately called "jealous James." His behavior at times left something to be desired and he deserved to be in Alternative Education. You could not visit the class without a hug from or a conversation with James. He would follow you like a puppy until you noticed him and his eyes would follow you throughout the room making certain that he was not missed. He had to speak to you, obviously had his feelings hurt if you didn't talk to him and loved the attention which it appeared he was not at all used to, at least in a positive way. James left us following sixth grade and continued to visit or call us regularly until he became an adult. There was no doubt that Alternative Education had left its positive mark on James.

In our efforts to succeed with these students we were hit, kicked, spit upon, cursed, and had a number of life threatening phone calls. It was not easy. We succeeded with some, failed miserably with others, and soon learned that if the parent, almost always only a single mother, supported us and what we were trying to do for her child, the child would learn and had a good chance for success. Some parents were adamant, however, consistently declaring that their children were unfairly put into this program which did not have anything to do with us and, in their opinion; they did not need such an academic arrangement. As a result, we lost some and know that at least two are now serving life terms for murder. Another was himself murdered as a teenager, and still another as a young adult. Others have been in and out of jail. Even those who had been incarcerated returned to see us. I remember Jose yelling from one end of the hall to the other as a 12 year old, "I love you, Mr. Towery," and then returning as an adult the day after he was released from jail, body covered with tattoos to see us. His comment, "I haven't made a good decision since I left here, but I love you guys and I know what you tried to do for me."

Joe was one of our greatest successes. On his second day at

ALTERNATIVE EDUCATION

Cameron his behavior was totally out of control. He was going to kill Dr. Reynolds. I was called to the classroom. For the first time in my career, we cleared the room, and I called the police on a fifth grader. Two policemen arrived shortly to find Joe still going to kill the teacher as well as both of the officers. This went on for some time. Dr. Reynolds asked me what I hoped would happen and I replied that they needed to put handcuffs on him and take him away. The police must have read my mind. That is exactly what happened, and Joe was taken in the police cruiser directly to a judge in the juvenile court. He ended up out of school for an extended period and we were told repeatedly that we did not have to take him back. He had previously been in the program only two days, and Dr. Reynolds and I decided to give Joe another try. From that day we never had another problem of any kind with Joe who went on to graduate from high school, attend Ohio State University, and earn a degree in engineering. He visited and talked to the class every year, telling his story and encouraging the students to take advantage of the program and their education.

Another and equally significant lesson was taking place with the other boys while the situation with Joe was taking place. Looking out of the windows in an adjacent classroom, mouths hanging open in disbelief, the boys seemed to realize that being thrown into a police car in handcuffs could happen to them in the same way. We sat them down when it was over and explained why we did what we did. The class listened attentively and then said to Dr. Reynolds and me, "You are brave, you took us that nobody else wanted and you made us good." They were on their way to success but still believed that their goodness was imposed by us and could not be initiated from within.

At one meeting with young Ronald, a fifth grader, who was about to enter the program, the individual conducting the meeting asked about his drug use. Before the child could respond, his mother eagerly began to relate Ronald's drug history. Later in the meeting Ronald's mother was asked about what else Ronald had been involved in, and she began to expose his frail body covered with tattoos. Ronald was twelve and very small and thin for his age. Mother was frantic realizing that Ronald was out of control. Unfortunately, Ronald did not get far beyond the sixth grade and since has been in and out of jail. When he is out, however, he faithfully comes to visit and we welcome him.

Through the years severe behavior issues occurred more frequently with students who were increasingly younger and younger, hence the need for a primary class. In the last several years, some of our most challenging students were in kindergarten and first grade. They came to school angry for reasons they did not understand. They often lacked the same social skills as the older students and had often experienced far too much in their short lives.

Alfredo, the cutest five year old you have ever seen, liked to hit and kick both students and adults until it became obvious that, for the safety of the other students, he would have to be removed from the regular class and placed into Alternative Education. When I asked him why he hit people he responded without thinking, "Daddy hits mommy when he gets mad."

Alex, a handsome five year old, was abandoned by his mother, left on a doorstep at birth and raised in a foster home until his dad could be found. Dad, all of a sudden became a single parent raising a five year old and working the night shift. Alex spent weeknights with a baby sitter and was only with Dad on weekends.

Thomas came as a kindergarten student after a tumultuous beginning. His hearing and speech impediments were so severe that he could not be understood and thus he acted aggressively, most likely out of frustration. Most of these little ones had good reason to be angry but it took its toll on their learning and their classmates. Mrs. Barnes and her assistant provided a special warm and loving atmosphere in the small class, and growth, both social and academic, occurred every day. All of the younger students we received were able to successfully return to regular classrooms. If we were able get to the behavior issues when students were young, the liklihood of future school success was greatly increased.

Sadly, Alternative Education classes continue to be filled almost entirely with black and recently, Latino males. Based on their actions and behavior, most of the kids we worked with needed the alternative instructional arrangement. The majority of these boys came from single parent, modest income, female dominated homes where mother worked to the point that little attention was paid to the child. As the situation with minority males in our Alternative Education classes consistently repeated itself every year, we became convinced that schools needed to take an increased role and increased responsibility in making certain that all youngsters felt accepted, worthy, and were both encouraged and counseled into making good decisions for themselves. All too often, most of our young black and Latino males saw themselves as "ones that nobody wanted" when they arrived. We worked daily to separate behavior from acceptance.

If not, we knew that Alternative Education classes would continue to be needed and increasingly youngsters would be put out of school or passed into the court system. The boys knew full well when their behavior was acceptable and when it was not, yet that did not cause them to behave appropriately. The first priority for our Alternative Education students was always to communicate that someone at the school cared for them and believed they could learn. Once that was established, they were often eager to please. We did not accept poor behavior, we consistently corrected it.

I recently asked Sammy, who was new to the program, how he was doing with Dr. Reynolds. He said he was doing "good" even though I knew that was not necessarily the case. I asked him why he had not done well at his last school. He immediately responded, "The teacher didn't like me much." Research supports the critical factor that the perception of being "liked" and appreciated by the teacher plays, especially in black and minority children.

Winston had been in the program a while and was doing well. I asked one day if he was ready to return to his base school. He said no, "The teachers there are mean." I replied that Dr. Reynolds was probably the strictest teacher he had ever experienced. His response, "I know, but she loves me." Once children experienced some degree of success, often for the first time, they did not want to leave. Likewise, schools often did not want them to return.

The goal of the Alternative Education Program was always to correct behaviors, boost academic skills and have children return to their base schools where, hopefully, their successes would continue. When children left, however, they also knew that if their behavior was not improved in old surroundings, they could be sent back to Alternative Education. Such was the case with DeJuan. He was dismissed as a third grader and returned to us as a fifth grader. When he arrived the second time it was like a celebration for him. He hugged everyone, smiled broadly and knew that he was in a safe environment where he would behave and be cared for again. DeJuan went to work, learned and continues to think of himself as successful.

What I learned:

- Caring and acceptance are critical to school success.
- Black and now Latino males dominate our behavioral programs.
- Dressing for success makes a difference beyond appearances.
- Kids often think that we are the ones who make them "good" and that it cannot or does not come from within themselves.

A Little United Nations

"At Cameron we are all
A very special family,
We come from different places from
All around the world,
From Viet Nam to Pakistan,
Mexico and Columbia too,
From India, Bolivia and Africa to name a few.
Everyone, lets join hands
And spread peace all throughout these lands
For this is our hope, the world to unite
And all the people to love and not fight,
Please help us to make this world a better place,
Please help us to make this world a better place,
Please help us to make this world a better place."

Cameron School Song
Written by Mrs. Jennifer Dawson, teacher

TOUCHED BY A CHILD

There was a time that life in our schools seemed far less complicated. Suddenly, almost without warning, we entered a period when changes came overnight. Each new day brought students from every corner of the world along with new customs, new cultures, new dress, new experiences and new opportunities. We called this diversity. Diversity was far more than skin color, customs or educational backgrounds. Diversity was a departure from what we long considered the norm. I remember some years ago Molly Freeman, an experienced and well respected first grade teacher, commenting that she hoped she never had a student that did not speak English because she would have no idea how to teach or reach that child. Just a few years later many, if not most, of her children had native languages other than English. In spite of language, customs etc., these children blossomed, succeeded and achieved every bit as well as those born in the United States.

When I arrived at Cameron our student population was half African American and half white. Through the years the population changed dramatically to the point that 70% of our families had a native language other than English. Students came from all corners of the globe, represented all continents, and had family backgrounds that ranged from the nieces of tribal chiefs in Sierra Leone seeking to escape the fighting in that country, to those that had never lived in a modern society. I was told by one Latino mother that the area where they lived in El Salvador was so rural that the children often did not wear clothes until they were four or five years old. Though the majority of our non-native English speaking students were Latino, it was a continual geography lesson as Brett, Bart and Bo taught us about their native Palau, an island nation that few of us could have located on a map. Abu spoke about his native

Djibouti, another country with which we were unfamiliar and Reymon told us about his experience driving from here to El Salvador with his dad. One young man from the Philippines, upon his arrival at our school, promptly and emphatically stated, "I like it here. In my last school I was the only one in my class that was not white."

I considered myself particularly fortunate to have had the opportunity to be a part of these conversations as indeed I realized that at Cameron we were truly global citizens. Such exposure caused me to recognize that every corner of the globe was within a few hours reach and that we were no longer isolated from even the most remote addresses. The rest of the world was here and we were part of it.

As I stood in the Indian long house in the restored Jamestown (Virginia) village with a group of fourth graders, Mery said to me, "This is just like the house I lived in El Salvador. It was made of sticks and we put mud between them. We had a dirt floor and we even had a hole in the roof to let the smoke out, but I live in a big house now." I was stunned as I thought about what she had said. Here was this charming little girl who was achieving well in school, yet coming from a background so very different from mine and that of so many of our American children. I had never thought about our students coming from places that I would have considered rather primitive by our standards.

We heard from Paul about his family's terrifying escape from Iran and from An and her brother Mohammed as she wrote: "I came in America because there is war in my country. When there is war in someone's country some people might die when they are fighting. Well at 5:00 a.m. some Russian soldiers came into our house. They came in and asked us where is your father. We did not answer. The soldiers started searching our house and found my father. They hit my father and mother with their guns. I remember that I was crying. But then I heard my father saying "Good-bye." Then I knew they were going to do something to my father. After a couple of days they mailed us a letter that said they killed my father. We were scared they might do something to us, too. So we decided to go to Pakistan. We did not go by plane, we went by horses. We had a hard time going to Pakistan. The mountains in Afghanistan has a lot of rocks. In five days and five nights we were on horses. After five days and five nights we arrived in Pakistan. We found a house there. We stayed there three years. Then we came to America. I came in here like the story says. I would like everyone to be friends, not like the Russians did to us. I have always wished that I had my father with me! So freedom is please always be friends."

Likewise Mohammed's dad told about being tortured because he was a civilian employee of the American Embassy in Kabul and how the family was kept safe in the embassy compound until they were able to come to the United States as refugees. They left both family and furnishings behind wondering if they would ever see any of them again. He told that having been a professional in his country, it was difficult to start over in America, raise five children on meager wages, and adapt to a new lifestyle.

As I read the newspaper daily or listened to the news, I was forced to think so many times that we adults should be like our children who came from every background, represented every religion, and spoke every language yet worked together in a school where all were friends and where none of their differences were important. We adults "messed it all up," the kids understood tolerance, friendship, caring and compassion.

Occasionally and most frequently in their writings, the children spoke of their experiences with war as especially terrifying. They could not escape it and were a part of what went on around them. A young scholar, Ahmed, brought pictures of his native Pakistan when he wrote his autobiography. The routine pictures of street scenes showed tanks, soldiers with guns and an obvious military presence. This was something not out of the ordinary for him as a child. I reflected, even looking back on 9-11, that theirs was a lifestyle that was still very unfamiliar to all of us. Jesus wrote that his family came to the Unites States from El Salvador when the gangs entered his home, took his father, and he never saw him again. We continually worked to help kids overcome their fears of gangs, shootings and wars which they brought with them from the past. Thankfully, here in America they felt they had less to fear and it seemed far less likely that someone would come into their home at any time and take some of their family members away forcefully.

Through my interaction with our immigrant children I realized every day that, to the outside world, America was a far greater nation than most of us that were raised here recognize. I heard and continue to hear countless stories from our children about the struggles of their families to get to the United States. Given the state of poverty and the lack of work in their home countries, I understood why they risked their lives to make a better existence for their families, to find work, often at menial jobs, food, education and opportunity. Eduardo, Jose and Angelina came to school one day and asked the staff to pray for their family, "We have to pray because Daddy is coming." A day or two later they told us, "We have to pray really hard today because daddy is getting close." The next day they reported that "Daddy made it" and still the next day, "Daddy is here and he's going to work tomorrow." We all celebrated with the children. Even with all the risks, families never hesitated to come. I will never forget one of our Instructional Assistants, a native of Mexico, as she commented tearfully to staff, "When I open my refrigerator, here in America there is always food. In Mexico that was not true."

I had the following conversation with a group of fifth grade boys at the lunch table late one spring. For whatever reason I asked Mario, a ten-year-old fifth grader who had been in the United States for about fifteen months, who he had come to the United States with. He replied, "No one. I came by myself." I said, "You came by yourself, you were a brave little boy to get on a plane by yourself and come to a new country not knowing anyone or knowing the language." He answered, "I didn't come on a plane." "How did you come, I wondered." "I walked," he said. He looked at me surprised that I did not already suspect his answer. "You walked here from El Salvador." "Uh huh". In my state of shock I asked, "How long did it take?" "Twenty-one days," he replied. I asked, "How many of you were there?" "Eight of us", he answered. "Did you know any of them?" I continued to question. "Not when we started," he said. "Where did you stay at night," I pursued with my questions. "There were people that kept us," he continued. "Were you scared?" I questioned. He replied, "A little bit but when I got here mom was there to meet me," he said proudly.

Mario was as fine a young man as ever anyone would want to

know. He told me that mom and dad had been here about three and a half years without him and how badly he missed them. I realized how risky it was for the parents to pay a "coyote" a large sum to bring their child to the United States, walking, not knowing if he would be killed, harmed, sexually abused or even knowing if they would ever see him again. I also came to the realization that the "Underground Railroad" continues today. Only once before in my years as principal did I ever have a child tell me that he had come into the United States in the trunk of someone's car.

For the sake of the children who didn't understand or weren't even aware of the immigration system, I wished I had answers to the immigration issues facing the United States. Yet, I was continually glad that I did not have to be the one to solve them. Even with no idea of the legal status of our Cameron families, when names and faces were put on the children, you looked at the situation very differently. Our children were some of the finest with whom I ever had the pleasure of working. They were diligent, appreciative, eager to learn, succeed and by and large excellent citizens. Indeed, many of our former students hoped to receive their permanent citizenship by serving in our military in Iraq and Afghanistan. They returned to school wearing the military uniform proudly. I received the following note from one of our former students from El Salvador now a Marine on the occasion of my retirement:

"Dear Mr. Towery I want to wish you a great life of retirement because you really deserve it. You have been such a wonderful person to me and everyone in my family. Starting from Jorge, and Fanny to me and Ana, to my Mom and Dad and lastly my Godchild, Miriam. I graduated in '08 and a month after

I went to boot camp. Miriam just graduated this year 2010 and is headed off to college. No matter what experiences I go through, I will always remember walking the hallways of Cameron Elementary and you always had a great big smile with open arms waiting for a hug. Take care and have a fantastic life. We love you. Love, Michael Garcia."

I remember the week Roman arrived as a fourth grader from the Philippines and my visit to his class several days later. As I entered the classroom, Roman immediately stood then, looking quite embarrassed, promptly sat down. I commented as to why he stood and he replied that in the Philippines students always stood as a form of respect when the teacher, director or an adult entered the room. Roman became a wonderful student and citizen. Several years ago I received a phone call in the office. When I picked up the receiver a familiar voice said, "Mr. Towery, this is Roman calling you from Fallujah, Iraq. I just wanted to talk to you." It was a very emotional moment for me. Several months later Roman came into the office in his dress uniform; a decorated United States Marine now serving in California. As a staff we were all incredibly proud.

Alfredo came to the United States speaking no English at all. In his first year he made remarkable progress and proved himself to be an excellent student. He participated in every school event and took advantage of every opportunity. The following year as summer school ended Alfredo told me one day that his cousin had come to the United States. I told him to bring the cousin to school. With the opening of school the cousin arrived. We were all shocked that the cousin could read English reasonably well. I commented to Alfredo that Carlos could read. He replied, "Every night I take my book home and every night I teach him to read." Such was the commitment of many of our non English speaking youngsters. Alfredo continued to be a success in high school and went on to college.

Several years after leaving Cameron, I received the following letter from the cousin, Carlos:

"Dear Mr. Towery,

I hope that when you receive my letter you are doing fine. Mr. Towery, you know I haven't forgotten you after all, of course you are the number one principal in the whole wide world.

So tell me how is everything doing there. I will never forget the day you said to me "You will always be special". I will never forget about Cameron Elementary School, the teachers, office staff, cafeteria staff, Mr. Fred (custodian) and of course you. I love all of you very much. Please tell them all that Carlos has not forgotten about them.

Well you know Junior High is not too bad. The principal is not as nice as you and the teachers are old. I have one teacher that is 61 years old.

Well I hope you will write me back soon and tell Ms. Mathers I said "Hi". Remember tell Mrs. Sackler, Mrs. Pence, and Mr. Hillary to write to me. I'll be waiting for your letter. Carlos Garcia"

Of course this was the reward for choosing to become a teacher and what made us love our jobs. Our students who came from other countries and their families were overwhelmingly appreciative of everything the school did for their children. They held the school and the teachers in such high regard that we often felt rewarded by their presence. As the students continued their education beyond elementary school, many success stories were shared with us. One included the organization of a Hispanic Leadership Club by former Cameron students at the local high school. The after school club was designed to encourage and inspire younger siblings and younger students to take advantage of the educational opportunities available to them. One of their leaders, Cindy Chavez, was awarded a scholarship to a prominent university, the result of her academic standing and her leadership in this group.

I was also struck that our non-English speaking parents attended every meeting, event or information session though they most often understood little of what was being said. Likewise, they relied on their children to translate, explain report cards, fill out school forms and whatever else was required in our large metropolitan area. While we were educating the children we were educating the families as well. Our Latino parents met monthly with our Parent Liaison, Mrs. Gonzales, who often arrived in the morning to find parents waiting for her. I always attended their monthly meetings which were as much social as educational. Though I didn't speak Spanish and was determined to learn, I had a good idea what was being discussed. At the end of the meeting the group always applauded me to show appreciation just for my having come to their meeting. Parents were so supportive, though they generally did not have a lot of money. One thing they enjoyed doing was feeding us their traditional food. They knew by our response that we liked and appreciated their delicious cooking. Annually, the Latino community hosted a huge luncheon for the staff. One of my favorite foods that through the years I came to know well was papusas, corn tortillas stuffed with chicken, cheese or meat. Served hot with slaw on top they were hard to beat. They were a real treat. In this way the parents were able to return their appreciation to the school.

Our reading specialist met every other Thursday morning with a group of Latino mothers and the Parent Liaison to work on ways they could help their children in reading. On one occasion the parents asked to take a field trip. They wanted to go to the library one Thursday morning to get library cards and to learn how the library worked. They were afraid to go by themselves for fear that they would not understand, not know what to ask or would be embarrassed by their lack of English. Many of our non-English speaking parents, especially those from the Central American countries, had little formal schooling themselves and were extremely anxious for their children to do well in school in the United States.

As we learned more about a student's background or culture we understood better the world around us. Our young man from Djibouti had a difficult time with his behavior, and we requested a conference with the parents. They graciously came, mother in her traditional dress, dad in a suit. As we spoke about Abu's behavior and the need for improvement, dad became very upset with Abu and began to scream at him, "If you don't behave we will send you back to our country to live as a nomad herding the sheep and the goats, living in a tent like our people do without ever a real place to live." I don't know if Abu believed him, but I was convinced that dad would do exactly that. I was also startled again to realize that backgrounds could be so different or even that people continued to live like that at this point in history.

Of course, there are the funny stories like the day Juan's mother called and asked one of us to go to Juan's classroom and see if he had brought granddad's false teeth to school for "show and tell." Granddad was visiting from Latin America. As you might expect, they were there. Sadly other families found themselves in poverty like the family of a young lady from one of the central African countries whose father remained in Africa and was one of the tribal leaders. Here she and her mother received nothing from him and lived a meager existence. One single American mother raised her own children and three others from Guatemala that were not hers. Grandpa Saeed was persistent; every time he was able to get enough money he would bring one more grandchild to the United States until he had the entire family in one place.

What a happy day it was for all of the staff when Patricia entered the office, resume in hand to apply for a teaching position. We remembered well Patricia, her brother and sister as hard working students. The father worked as a waiter at a local restaurant and mother cleaned houses. Patricia had become a teacher, Luis, her brother, was a college graduate and an engineer and younger sister was in college. The American dream lived and hard work was still rewarded.

One of our third graders from Ghana brought with him the game of bottle caps which obviously had a great deal of meaning to him. One recent school year found large groups of upper grade boys spread out on the floor in the gym in the morning before class shooting and trading bottle caps. Students carried their caps in everything from paper bags, and backpacks to special "treasure boxes", always careful not to lose their "keepers." I never completely understood the game but it was intense. I wondered how many places you could go in this country and find children and their parents offended that children would resort to playing with bottle caps. It had to be fun and required some skill in shooting yours further than the other students.

I asked Sergio, a sixth grader, when school opened in the fall what he had done over the summer. He told me that he had spent much of the summer in Honduras with his grandmother. I asked if he had a good time. He told me that he was glad to see grandma but that he wouldn't want to live there. He said that he couldn't sleep because he could see the rats running across the rafters in the house at night, and he was afraid of them. He also said he couldn't eat because grandma would go out, get a chicken, swing it around to break its neck, then skin it and cook it. One day, he said it was his turn to get the chicken but he couldn't kill it, he only managed to break its leg. He was glad to come back home. Again I realized the extreme differences in backgrounds and cultures that our children represented. While students from the middle or upper middle class society went to Disney World or went on cruises with their parents for vacation, many of ours had radically different experiences.

I recently received the following note from one of our Latino parents:
"Mr. Towery: When I arrived in this country, I didn't believe that my son Alex Moreno and I could find a very good school but we did. The most important point in a school is the principal. Mr. Towery you are always a good leader in the school

and the best friend to all the students. CAMERON is always like our house. Alex and I always have all of you in our hearts. Thank you Victoria Saycho"

What I learned:

- Everyone has a story to tell.
- Customs and lifestyles that I imagined had long passed into history still thrive in some parts of the world.
- The United States of America is a wonderful place and how fortunate I am to have been born here.
- Children don't see differences in each other; they see similarities.
- Those families that arrived in the United States recently often have a greater appreciation for our blessings than do we.

Po-Verty

Both at Lorton and at Cameron, in addition to the students who received free or reduced lunch, we were constantly aware through a variety of means that in many of our homes there was little extra money. Families struggled to provide the best for their children and we worked to support their efforts. Andre was the hidden child who could not tell us where he lived although we knew well. His brother and sister lived in an apartment with their mother and so did he. Andre, however, was the hidden child and the oldest, a third grader. Mother rented an apartment where she was allowed only two children because of the sexes of the children and the number of bedrooms, and she had three children. As a result, Andre was given the responsibility of keeping his place of residence a secret because if he told, they would get "put out". Unfortunately, the responsibility of not getting "put out" was all placed on Andre, and if the family was found out Andre would carry all the blame. Because of poverty, children often became tangled in the issues of the adult world which they frequently did not understand.

LaToya in second grade was the youngest of Mrs. Jackson's children and the only girl. LaToya did not like to leave her mama and come to school. As a result her attendance was poor, and her achievement well below where it should have been. I decided it was time to make a home visit to the tiny duplex one day and talk with Mrs. Dunn about getting LaToya to come to school regularly. I was welcomed warmly and sat on the couch. I soon realized that the house was completely infested with roaches. As I tried to carry on a conversation, I was distracted as the roaches were coming down the walls, across the floor, and up the side of the couch where I was sitting. I visited some pretty filthy houses in my home visits but that was the only time I was ever chased out by roaches. Nonetheless, it was a very short conversation. Children who came from homes where the family was poor were often forced to live in substandard conditions detrimental to their health and that of the family. Further, families were often very careless in their care of the rental property. Likewise, it was difficult to get the landlord to make repairs and do proper maintenance. As for the kids, they were caught in the middle of a cycle over which they had little or no control.

Sixth grade Tony needed a ride home from school one day, and the job fell to me as I was going his way when I left the building. As we drove the short drive to Tony's house, he complained about how hungry he was. I listened, but as I had to return to school later in the evening, I told him that I was certain that when mom got home from work she would fix dinner. We arrived at their rather nice townhouse to find mom already home and I remarked, "Good, mom is home so you will have dinner soon." The next morning I happened to see Tony and I asked him what he had for dinner. He replied that he had cereal as that was the only food they had in the house. I knew that mom struggled financially and that raising her three children in a decent housing area was important to her. It never before occurred to me that families that lived in nice houses did not always have what they needed. We had passed McDonalds on the way to Tony's house. Had I known there was no food in the house I would have made certain that he was fed. On several other occasions when I drove Tony home, I always asked if he was hungry and needed something to eat.

Kindergarten Walter, tiny and frail, cried often because his breakfast was twenty cents and he only had ten cents or nothing. One of us routinely dug into our pockets to see that Walter had breakfast. We were also quick to learn that the school breakfast was very important to getting his day started well and was certainly a higher priority than reading or math. For many of our children the school breakfast and lunch was the mainstay of their diet. When children came to school late and checked in at the office they often asked the secretary, "Is breakfast over?" Even if it was, we did our best to see that they were fed before they went to class. Every day at lunch time children asked, almost begged, to have another hot dog, slice of pizza, some extra spaghetti or anything else to eat.

Joshua, a first grader, arrived from another school system in our metropolitan area. He entered daily with a ring of white crust from the previous night's saliva dried around his mouth. Once at school his first priority was not learning to read and write or even going to class. The first issue every day was, "What's for breakfast?" and "How much can I have?" Joshua was always dirty, hair uncut and uncombed, full of little lint balls.

Strangers that did not know him thought he was a girl. Joshua said he slept on the floor and there were no mattresses. We believed the floor to be the source of the lint and trash in his hair. His used school uniforms, provided by the school, were a mass of wrinkles as though he had slept in them. When he registered, mother was given a bag of clothes for Joshua and his little brother from the clothing center which she much appreciated. Mother said the family did not have a place to live and were staying with friends. There was evidently no income and whatever Joshua needed for school was provided by the school. Even around youngsters that had little, Joshua stood out as his general appearance told his story.

As middle class Americans with full cupboards, we most always assumed that families had sufficient food in their kitchens to prevent their children from being hungry. After all this was the United States. Yet when you daily watched children collecting the unopened cartons of milk in the cafeteria to take home you had to be suspicious. Likewise when children came to school on the very first day and were disappointed to learn that there was no breakfast until the second or third day of school, you realized how much the school's food was relied on. Lots of the adults packed or took their lunches to school as we preferred not to purchase the school food. However, children frequently told us how wonderful the food at school was and how much they liked it. As you watched them dispose of their trash as they were returning to class, you realized that there was little thrown away.

One of the most significant days of the school year was the day at the end of the month of September when the free and reduced lunch from the previous year expired. Children of parents who had not sumitted a new form found themselves suddenly without the two meals they so depended on. The Assistant Principal, Parent Liaison and I began on the first day of school encouraging and assisting parents as they completed the new form so their children didn't find themselves without at the end of the month. Most parents complied, but there were always tears as we scrambled to find something for the children to eat until the new form was submitted and approved.

Susie and Jason were twin second graders from a seemingly middle class home who lived with mom and dad. Dad worked every day but mom had problems with drugs. Almost every other morning one of the twins called the office to say, "Mom won't get up again, but we want to come to school. Can you come and get us?" One of us, usually the secretary, assistant principal or I made the short drive to pick them up. The kids were ready and waiting having gotten themselves up and dressed. We went so frequently that our car almost drove the route by itself. Dad was open and honest with us explaining the he simply could not miss work and that he knew well mom's issues and was trying to address them. He was greatly appreciative of the school's efforts to transport, feed and care for his children.

Aaron and his second grade brother shared a winter coat. One wore it one day and one the next. Thanks to donations from churches, organizations and individuals we were able to provide coats for Aaron and his brother. We also maintained food cards for families in the office and clothes in the Clothing Center. As our cabinets at home were full of food we continued to be surprised when folks like Mrs. Johnson came in to tell us that she had nothing in her cabinets except a bag of rice or Mrs. Williams said that she had absolutely nothing to feed her children tonight, could we help her? One mother came to the Clothing Center barefooted and would have taken anything we would have given her. Children deserve to have food in their tummies, warm coats on their backs and focused best on learning when those needs were met. Any assistance we gave families was always very much appreciated. I have always believed that every child in these United States regardless of their circumstances should receive a free hot lunch at school every day.

The following notes were received after a local church group sponsored a Christmas shopping trip for our children:
"Thanks so much for those responsible for choosing Timmy as one of those selected for the shopping trip. It was a great help and boosted his self esteem too. Although a girl's death prompted this fund, it's always nice to see something good come from something bad that happened Yours truly, Martha Miller and Timmy"

"Dear Mr. Towery, My name is John Beasley. I was one of the "helpers" on Dec. 10 for the students of your school as they shopped at K-Mart for Christmas presents. Specifically, I was the helper of Nathan, a sixth grader from your school. I don't know his last name, and I would like to send him a card. Could you call me or send me his name and address so I can do so?

That Saturday was the first time I had ever been involved in a program of its kind. After that Saturday morning, I realized that this is truly a shame. Mr. Towery, I have never been so touched or humbled as I was after spending time with Nathan. For only being 12 years old, he has lived through harder times than any of my friends or I have even come close to experiencing. Nathan made me truly appreciate what I have.

Sincerely, John Beasley

Once again it would be greatly appreciated if you could call or write to me with the information I need on Nathan. My address is ...."

"Miss Raymond Would you know of any way I could get some help so my kids could have a little for xmas. My husbane he work tree work and he don't get much work in the winter. I would not ask but I don't see any way of getting them anything Mrs Allen"

Tiny third grade Sean had severe asthma. His attacks were so severe and so frequent that 911 was repeatedly called. We as a staff were terrified and often prayed that he would survive until the medics arrived. We were justifiably scared for him. Teachers were very careful in deciding whether he should be allowed out to recess on hot and humid days though he always wanted to go and would even sneak out if he could. Sean would arrive in the clinic gasping for breath, his chest heaving from the difficulty he had breathing. In spite of his well known condition, the school was never given any form of medication or provided with any suggestions for treatment other than calling 911. Most school age children in Virginia were able to qualify for some form of insurance; however, medication was a different story. If there were multiple children in the family and money for the basic necessities of food and rent were scarce, the prescription went unfilled.

Stringy-haired first grade Xavier was determined to run away from school. His teacher, Ms. Rose and I decided we needed to take him home and have a talk with mother. As we pulled up to the house a well-dressed couple was going in. I knocked at the door and a baby clad only in a diaper opened the door to let us in. We smiled at the other couple sitting in chairs across from us. As soon as Xavier ran upstairs mother began to scream "WHAT'S THIS SH.., WHAT'S THIS SH.." Mother came half way down and sat on the stairs wearing a very skimpy negligee. As we tried to talk, there was a knock at the door. No one made any attempt to answer it. I finally got up and opened the door and a well dressed gentleman in a suit and tie came in and sat in the only other chair in the room. We smiled. Mother proceeded to tell us that we could do anything to Xavier we wanted or needed to in school, but absolutely he was not to be brought home. At that point a man dressed in pajama pants wandered through the living room and went upstairs without saying anything. The last man to arrive got up and asked if he could go upstairs also. Ms. Rose and I looked at each other and decided that it was time for us to leave, with Xavier. Two days later there was a half million dollar drug bust at the home and we never saw Xavier again.

Rocky's, Jamie's and Rita's fathers were in jail and Sarah's mother was in jail. These were just a few of our children who had parents in jail. Children from poverty knew the word jail well. They visited as often as they could, or they seldom visited at all and wished they could see mom or dad more often. A parent in jail reduced family income and created additional hardships for kids. In addition, it created the stigma that, "My parent's in jail." The guardian, most always with meager resources, was pushed to provide the basics as nothing in the form of financial resources came in when one or the other parent was locked up.

Pressures on poor parents easily rose to the breaking point if there were problems, either academic or behavioral, in school. Parents feared us calling because they frequently saw themselves as helpless in doing anything about the problem other than beating the child. Tim's mother arrived in tears after a phone call home and told me that she had driven around the Washington beltway three times before she could calm down and finally told me just to "beat him any way I wanted" because she just couldn't deal with him.

Elliott lived in a shelter, so did Mary. Elliott's family lost their apartment after dad went to jail and Mary's mother lost her apartment after she lost her job. Neither family had anywhere else to go. Our children knew and understood shelters: Meals were served at one time and if you were not there, you didn't eat. If you didn't follow their rules you were "put out." You stayed only as long as two weeks. The people in the next room were always "making trouble for us." We heard those comments often from our children who seemed to take it in stride and survived much better under the circumstances than we would. At least most shelters provided a quiet time for doing homework. Mark, Bonnie and Jeremy lived in Room 32 of the Fireside Motel because all of the shelters were full. They had two double beds, a cot, a microwave and a compact refrigerator. Dad was looking for a job while the kids' lives were in confusion.

Many children found their lives and thus their education seriously impacted by frequent or constant moves. Research tells us that a mid-year change in schools can set a child back as much as half a year in their academic work. One child, as a result of multiple moves, came to us after spending three years in first grade never having completed any of them.

Alfredo's family came from Honduras only to find everything much more expensive than they expected and the lack of basic English a problem in trying to get assistance. Finding housing, finding work, providing the basics were all often more difficult than many immigrant families expected when they arrived. Alfredo, age 13, talked every day about getting a job so he could help dad with the bills. He believed that McDonalds would hire him when he was fourteen. In Honduras, Alfredo knew he could have found a job at age thirteen. Alejandro, Merriam, Diana and Fidel lived in a basement apartment with three babies and five other adults. They had no furniture only mattresses. The adults who were not working at the moment cared for all of the kids. There was no place to do schoolwork and the rules of the house changed depending on what adult was in charge at the time. A change in home environment was difficult for all children, even those born in the United States and moving from a rural to an urban area where families lived in close proximity to each other.

If a family met the Federal income guidelines based on the information they provided on the annual Free and Reduced Lunch form, they were determined to be impoverished. Based on the numbers of students who received free or reduced lunch or breakfast, schools were allocated Title 1 funding from the Federal Government to support the school. Approximately 65% of our students fell in the free and reduced category.

Though the Federal Government considered them to be poor, the students certainly thought differently.

While children from situations of poverty lacked many of the resources of middle class children, they often had resources that astounded us. Tyrone, fifth grade, came to school with a pager that went off repeatedly during the day. I called mother to report it. Mother told me that he was carrying a big knife also. Tyrone said that he carried the knife to protect himself. We felt certain that the pager was the mother's who we believed was selling drugs and was using Tyrone as the go between because a child would not likely be suspected. On another occasion, a group of fourth graders were caught shoplifting at the local mall. In listening to their story, they were eager to share how easy it was and how good they were at it.

As I worked with a fifth grade reading group, we read the story, "Beauty and the Beast." In the story Beauty's father lost all of his money and sank into poverty. Each time I read the story with a group, the children would ask, "Mr. Towery, what's poverty"? (which they pronounced po-verty). My standard reply was that poverty was when you were poor and didn't have enough money to meet all of your families needs. In turn I asked them who they knew that lived in poverty. After much thought and discussion, they agreed that the homeless people on the streets were the people in poverty. Never did the students relate poverty to themselves in any way, though in conversation they frequently said that, "Mama said there was no money" for this or that in the household. Poverty to us, was very different from poverty to them.

What I learned:

- The experiences of children living in poverty are different from those of middle class children.
- The appearance of the house on the outside is not always an indication of what is in the kitchen.
- School breakfast and lunch are essential to school success and often the most important part of the school day.
- Children from poverty carry more of the weight of the world than do other children.
- Children from poverty don't wear signs that read "My family is poor."

"There's 12 Towels in the Bathroom and they're All Clean"

I returned from Disney World with my family at spring break one year and promptly asked a class of sixth graders on the first morning back how they enjoyed their time off. They responded in unison with a resounding "BORING". It was quickly obvious to me that while different staff had done everything from Disney World to Caribbean cruises, most of our children had spent their time in front of television sets or video games, often at home by themselves, and had done nothing.

Our school trips were especially significant to the kids which they usually regarded as "vacation." Trips gave the staff lots of insights to the students. We took first through third graders camping one night, fifth and sixth graders two nights. Fourth grade went to the State Fair in Richmond and to Jamestown and Williamsburg. The sixth grade traveled to New York at the end of the school year. This became known as, "The Sixth Grade Trip." Wherever we went, it was a first time experience for many of the children and most of the parents as well. The questions asked and the comments made on every trip never ceased to be fascinating.

Camping was an annual treat to the 4-H center at Front Royal in the mountains or another local camp about 80 miles from home. Students really became excited about camping, and first timers would run around the school constantly telling the adults, "I'm going camping, I'm going camping, What's camping?" You began to realize that though the students knew this was going to be a "fun experience," they had no idea at all what camping was about. As we were on our way driving along the interstate in a highway bus and at the foot of the mountains one of the sixth grade girls asked me, "Is this the country?" On another occasion as the bus went along sixth grade Michael, who could succeed in any Gifted Talented class, asked, "What is that?" pointing to a large animal that was grazing in the field. One of the other children quickly replied, "It is a cow?" to which Michael responded, "I have never seen a live cow before?" That led to a delightful conversation about what colors "cows come in" and lots of laughter. On still another occasion as the bus traveled through the countryside, sixth grade Isaiah asked, "What are those?" pointing to large animals lazily strolling through a large field. Another student promptly replied "cows." Isaiah was quick to ask, "Are they real?" to which the second student said, "I don't think anyone would put fake cows in a field." As an adult I was shocked to realize that twelve year olds could not identify cows grazing in the field.

Arriving at camp and taking your "stuff" to your room was exciting. Students were awed with their surroundings and the natural beauty of the area. On many occasions I was told,

"This is the most beautiful place I have ever seen." Teachers were also excited about the trips and worked tirelessly organizing and presenting many curriculum related lessons but in an entirely different atmosphere. We invited special guests like the planetarium director at the local high school who set up a night time study of the stars and the "YoYo Man" who presented every child with a Yoyo then proceeded to teach them what to do with it.

Parents, and there were many that accompanied the group, looked at this as vacation too. As teachers worked with rotating groups of kids, parents listened and worked right along learning with their children. Obviously, if children had not been given the opportunity to get away from home, parents hadn't either. Relationships built between staff and parents were invaluable as parents appreciated and experienced first hand the skill and hard work of teachers and their love and care of the children.

Everything about camping was special, especially mealtime. Though the staff did not prepare the food, parents and staff worked together on the serving line serving the children. The very notion that, "You can get all you want", or that "You can go back for seconds", was a broad departure from school lunch and children took every advantage of the invitation to have "seconds" or thirds or fourths. I suspect some of the children were really full for the first time in a long time.

After dinner children looked forward to dancing the Chicken Dance and "Down the River" which could go on and on, singing silly camping songs like "Little Bunny Foo Foo" and "John Brown's Ford." The highlight of the evening was the nightly campfire and of course those "smores" (graham crackers stuffed with roasted marshmallows and placed on a Hershey chocolate bar). The crowning touch of the evening was Mr. Hillary's, the Assistant Principal's, scary story, "Bloody Fingers", completely made up as he told it and asked for again and again regardless of how many previous camping trips students had been on or how many times they had heard it.

For each of us there were those memorable moments camping like the year there were snakes everywhere, and we were afraid someone would get too close. Of course, the only ones who seemed intimidated were the adults. There was the year the bat flew into the high ceilinged auditorium where we were singing so as we sang our heads constantly moved following the flight pattern of the bat which seemed totally uninterested in us and caused no harm. As we ate dinner one night, one of the teachers remarked that there was a black bear outside of the dining hall. Every child ran toward the windows and hearing the noise, the bear quickly left the area. We reminded the students that bears are not pets and should they see one, remember to stay away. One year I had been ill and could not attend and as a result received the following:

"Hi, Mr. Towery! Happy birthday to you! I wish you get better. The trip was perfect. I loved this trip very much. Only one thing was bad-that you weren't with us. I saw many wild animals. Deer bears and chipmunks were here. I saw many interesting kinds of birds like hawks falcons and owls. Camping trip was just fine. We went to the caverns. The guide told us about fish, water, rocks and bats. Yesterday we had a campfire. We sang played games and ate marshmallows. I never got bored on the trip. It was fun. I wish you had a happy birthday and

that all of your dreams come true. Goodbye Leo P.S. We miss
you"

"Dear Mr.T Hello! Everythings fine at camp! Everyone had a
great time! But the food wasn't the best. The caverns were the
best. But Mrs. Rogers (Mary's mom) got sick. But she's fine.
Some people climbed Hawksbill Mountain. Other people took
a hike on the nature trail. Mr. Albertson is an old fart! I'm sorry
but it's true. I'm sure a lot of the people agree. Two people that
live in the 4-H place told a local horror story. I don't believe
them. Mary and I had a duck adventure. Have a happy happy
birthday!! Your Secret Student!"

"Happy Birthday Mr. Towery: How are you? We are fine, on
Monday I went to Skyline Caverns, in Skyline Caverns I saw
water estalacmites and estalactites. My room is number 30, I
sleep with Leo, Andy and James; all the nights I shower and
brush my teeth. We eat breakfast, lunch and dinner. Well bye
Mr. Towery and Happy Birthday. The End Julio"

The year that I had seven or eight sixth grade boys in my
group who shared two rooms connected by doors made a lasting impression. As we prepared for bed Solomon, one of the
sixth graders from the Congo said, "Get to your knees guys,"
to which the others responded, "What are we going to do?"
"We are going to pray!," he stated emphatically, and all quickly knelt as he instructed. Solomon prayed one of the most
beautiful prayers I can ever remember having been a part of,
thanking God for the staff, the place and for the opportunity
to participate in this wonderful camping event. I was deeply
moved by this experience as it spoke to the kind of person
Solomon was becoming. Solomon certainly set himself up as

a leader and later became our SCA President. On another occasion as we put the little ones to bed, I instructed the children that it was time to put their pajamas on and go to bed. One came up and said to me, "I don't have any piyamas but can I go to bed anyway?"

This letter from Tim Tucker was truly special and spoke to the importance kids paid to camping:

"Dear Mr. Towery,

I have got to go camping. Please let me go. I love camping so much and I want to go with my friends. I have apologized to you and Mrs. Thompson and I have, and will be good since that day.

Mr. Towery this means everything to me. I am sincere in saying I'm sorry. I know it was wrong but I have been good . I really want to go so please reconsider. I will be good the rest of the year and if you want me to do anything to help like cleaning up rooms and stuff like that I will.

I also think a reminder is that all year when you or Mrs. Rush, Mrs. Thompson, Mrs. Mrs. Dillon and Mrs. Fitzgerald have asked for any help I have. Please let me go. I want to go more than anything. I'm very sincere, My number is..........so you can call me and let me know. I would love it more than anything If I could end my three great years at Cameron by being fortunate enough to go camping. Please, I am very sorry. Very Sincerely, Tim Tucker"

The Virginia State Fair was held annually the last week in September with a hub bub of exciting activity. The fair included numerous displays about the history of Virginia, products of the Commonwealth, all sorts of farm animals large and small and special shows or performances. The fourth graders took it all in, especially the animals. The children enjoyed watching one of the several cows that gave birth daily and the silly little ducks that repeatedly ran up a set of steps, ate, and then slid down a ramp only to do it over and over again. As the children wandered through the displays, the boys were especially fascinated by the Army "stuff" asking every sort of question about what Army men do, pretending they were "Army men," and collecting every handout and "give away" which they would later carry home. At the displays on wildlife students identified and held the snakes. In the historical area children rode in the ox cart and talked with "real" Native Americans. One of the highlights was the pig races with every student hoping they would be selected to be a "pig rooter" and have a chance to win an assortment of silly mementos. All were surprised when it was time for the pot bellied pig race, and as the gate opened the fat rascals just stood there and very slowly meandered around the track. There was much hilarious laughter.

As we arrived at the hotel one year Alejandro, who happened to be in my group, asked if the kids got to stay in the hotel with the adults or did the kids have to sleep in the bus. Surprised that he had asked such a question, I told him that the kids got to sleep in the hotel. When we entered the room, Alejandro walked all around studying everything and finally said to me, "Mr. Towery, there are sixteen towels in the bathroom." At that point it was evident that taking a trip and spending the night in a hotel was an entirely new and wonderful experience for Alejandro. On another occasion I remember Van who stated as we entered the hotel, "This is the most beautiful room I have ever seen." It was not the Ritz, likely the Days Inn or Quality Inn, but nonetheless beautiful to him and I am sure to many others. Later at the hotel in Williamsburg fourth grade Jennifer exclaimed with excitement, "There's twelve towels in the bathroom, and they're all clean." Little things that we wouldn't even consider made a real impression on kids who often found themselves in different circumstances.

The second day students listened attentively to the tour guide at the State Capitol, admired Hudon's statue of George Washington, and sat in the chairs of our legislators. At the Civil War iron works they pretended to fire the canon, dressed up like soldiers and listened to stories as to the role of men, women and children, both black and white, as the Civil War all but destroyed the City of Richmond. It was on to lunch and then home. Lunch was usually at Shoney's or the Ponderosa where students shared the buffet, which they pronounced buff-it. On every trip one of the first questions the kids asked was whether or not the lunch and dinner were buff-its.

My personal favorite trip was Jamestown and Williamsburg with the fourth grade. The children had read about the arrival of the colonists at Jamestown and now got to see the James River, the reconstructed fort and the original site first hand. One year as we were standing on the bank of the James River, Louie, who had recently arrived from the Philippines, asked me, "Was the Vietnam war fought around here?" followed by, "Do you know Rambo?" Hopefully the trip helped get a little bit of history straightened out for him.

As we walked the streets of Colonial Williamsburg, sat in the old State Capitol, and watched the blacksmith as he pounded the hot iron, wide eyed children took it all in. At the Capitol, the guide's reenactment of a trial for a lady charged with stealing and the explanation of the historical events that took place in that very room, helped our students, especially those from other countries and cultures, better understand what the United States was all about, what our freedom cost and what it means for us today. Standing on the parade field on George Washington's birthday watching him review the troops, at least one child asked, "Is that the real George Washington?" Every child wanted his or her picture taken in the stocks outside of the courthouse so they could show mom and dad back home.

In the evening, we walked the streets with a lantern (spelled lanthorn). The children visited craft shops and watched the printer print the "Virginia Gazette" or the wig maker powder a wig. Each event opened a new door of learning and understanding for our children. As I stated earlier, many of our children had few experiences. On one recent occasion as we walked the Duke of Gloucester Street in Colonial Williamsburg I asked the group who they thought might have walked this very street. Expecting to hear George Washington, Thomas Jefferson, etc., I was surprised to hear from one young man, "I dunno, King Tut, maybe." Sadly, I think he was telling the truth.

On the first day of school, the question on the minds of the sixth graders was, "Are we going to New York this year?" such was the significance of this Cameron tradition. We generally visited the United Nations, the Intrepid aircraft carrier, NBC studios, the Top of the Rock and had lunch in the food court at Grand Central Station. We ended our day at the South Street

Seaport where the children really got a taste of New York City. The second day we visited Ellis Island, the Statue of Liberty and the Liberty Science Center. Until 9-11 we annually went to the top of the World Trade Center. Now, sadly, we just visit the hole where it used to be.

At the United Nations, the tour guide always mentioned UN projects in different countries, some of which were the homelands of different ones of the children. Children were also particularly struck by the statue from Hiroshima, the front looking natural and the rear charred, destroyed from the heat and blast of the atomic bomb. The height of the buildings was always mesmerizing, especially on clear days, to children who had never seen buildings as tall as those. The kids could not wait to get in those "fast" elevators to the top so they could "Wow" and "Oh" and "Ah" over what they saw. NBC Studios was a favorite as the children were often much more familiar with the various shows than we adults. Always asked was, "Is this really where" this show or that comes from?

Ending the day at South Street Seaport children were reminded in advance that the five dollar gold necklaces and bracelets sold by the roving illegal street vendors were not real and would turn your neck green. Likewise, they were not going to buy a Rolex watch for fifteen dollars. Yet, when we arrived back at the bus, many proudly displayed their purchases, showed off their watches with bands that were much too large for a sixth grader's wrist, adorned themselves with gaudy jewelry, and made comments like, "I only paid $ 12 for mine and you paid $ 15."

Ellis Island produced a play each year where three or so actors portrayed the lives and stories of people who entered the United

States through Ellis Island. In this short play the struggles of families, issues in the home country, and the trials of separation were vividly portrayed. Our children sat silent, spellbound, often with tears in their eyes as they related these stories to the struggles of their own families and their own homelands today. On one occasion at the end of the performance an elderly woman in the audience stood, indicated that she was a retired school principal, and explained that she had entered the United States at Ellis Island from Ireland as a young child. That seemed to make everything real.

The Statue of Liberty has always stood out to all of us as one of America's most recognizable treasures and symbols. Children were anxious to go inside and climb as far up as time would allow. The New York harbor was itself impressive as children watched the ocean going ships and freighters pass. What a happy way to end the school year and to end the elementary school experience for our youngsters!

Michael Preston remembered his trip this way: "Dear Mr. Towery,

What I remember most about my year was our trip to New York. I had never been anywhere and was so excited to go to the World Trade Center and the Statue of Liberty. It was something I will always remember. I also remember the bus driver got a speeding ticket on the way up and you asked everyone to pitch in a dollar to help cover the cost. That's just the kind of guy you are! I also remember staying after school to jump rope to raise money for charity and you coming over the loudspeaker and saying the President Reagan had been shot-and giving us updates throughout the afternoon. But what I remember most was the human dynamo Mr. Towery, always positive, supportive and caring. Just the kind of role model I needed. I could write a lot more but I'm running out of space. Thanks for touching so many children's lives. Michael Preston"

We were often asked why we made all of these trips and took our kids so many places. First, we did not do anything that we did not like ourselves. The trips, though often tiring, were fun for us as well. Many of us visited these historic and beautiful places over and over, but watching the joy and excitement of the children made it all worthwhile and fresh every year. We recognized again and again that through our trips the world was being opened up to our students as they were given the opportunity to get out of their community and see the world. If they were going to aspire to become the doctors, teachers and leaders of the future, they needed to explore the world and see for themselves something outside of the world of television, video games and their immediate community.

As educators, we clearly and repeatedly learned that children from meager economic situations were just as bright, just as capable and could score just as well on achievement tests as children from much more affluent backgrounds. The difference was their lack of experiences. Though many were born here and still others immigrated to the United States by a host of means, from week to week our children seldom left their immediate surroundings. Although the Metro system cut through the center of our community, to our children it was completely foreign. When we made an annual evening family trip to the Smithsonian Air and Space Museum, it was as exciting for the parents as it was for the kids. Because of the lack of spoken English or the business of work, few of our families ever traveled the six or so miles into the Nation's capital to see, learn and enjoy the sights there. They were deeply appreciative of the opportunities offered them.

What I learned:

- Watching the joy of the children makes everything worthwhile.
- Our children suffered daily from a severe lack of experiences.
- Children love all you can eat restaurants, especially "buffits."
- Visiting our most significant monuments and symbols of our culture like Jamestown, Williamsburg and the Statue of Liberty never gets old.
- Tim Tucker really wanted to go camping (he did).

"School with a Barnyard"

(Fairfax Journal Newspaper Headline, May 6, 1998)

Traveler was a big silver rabbit. Cameron was a gray tabby cat. Both Traveler and Cameron along with a menagerie of critters lived and thrived at Cameron School. The Goat Project at Lorton not only became an excellent learning experience for the students in the Goat Club, but the goats were immensely enjoyed and appreciated by the entire student body and the community. It seemed reasonable when I arrived at Cameron, we should provide some animals for our students as well. After all, the school had a large courtyard that contained nothing but weeds and was never used for any purpose. This was a perfect place for animals.

Animals and kids go together. Every child, and most adults, love a kitten, a baby bunny, a recently hatched chick or duckling. A hostile, angry child could often be calmed by cuddling or taking care of an animal. Those children who did not or could not have pets were often those that needed and wanted to be around them the most. Taking a class to the courtyard at lunchtime became a pastime.

The Cameron community was vastly different from that of Lorton. Folks lived close together. Many students lived in high rise apartment buildings. Families rented residences and were not allowed pets. Soon after I arrived we began the Rabbit Club which every older boy wanted to be a part of. Girls were welcomed too but were a little more reluctant to join. We met after school and again, thanks to the 4-H, we began to learn about rabbits. With the help of some fathers we built some sturdy cages and purchased several rabbits. As interest grew and rabbits multiplied, though not as often as literature would have you believe they do, many of the students got rabbits of their own.

One day I received a phone call from a lady who worked with one of our parents. She indicated that they were a military family and had been transferred overseas. They had a large silver rabbit in need of a home. Indeed she said the rabbit was potty trained and would return to his cage to use the bathroom. Traveler quickly became a part of Cameron School. As she seemed to have told the truth about his potty training, we decided to let him live indoors rather than in the courtyard like the other rabbits.

One of the classrooms kept the cage and Traveler was allowed to run loose in the school. On one occasion we had a very elderly substitute in one of our upper grade classes. Quite surprised by what she thought she saw, she quickly went to the teacher in the next room and remarked, "Honey, I thought I saw a rabbit going down the hall." The reply, "You did." The teacher explained to her that Traveler was very much a part of our school. If there was such a thing as "one in a million," Traveler was the "one in a million" rabbit. He was large in size but the sweetest, most gentle rabbit. He never scratched or bit. He was a favorite of the kindergarten children who would carry him around holding him in every way but the right way. In the housekeeping center they dressed him up in baby clothes and wheeled him into the cafeteria or around the school in the little doll carriage. He just sat there and seemed to enjoy the children and his surroundings. After a wonderful life, Traveler died of old age at Cameron.

Everyone loved the rabbits, but they had to be kept in cages. Just like Traveler, a neighbor of the school called after Easter and offered us a duckling. We were hooked, went out and purchased a kiddie pool and watched as the duck grew and had the run of the courtyard. We soon learned that ducks were cute, but ducks were messy. One of the classes decided that they would like to hatch some baby chicks. The hatching was successful and some of the chicks remained, grew and lived in the courtyard. As a city boy, I never had a close encounter with a chicken but soon learned that, except for an occasional rooster, they were quite entertaining and a lot of fun. As my office faced the courtyard, I learned that a chicken on my windowsill bobbing its head up and down would quickly diffuse an angry parent who seemed to find it difficult to rant and rave while being studied by a chicken.

Like Traveler, the children adored the chickens which could easily be picked up and carried around. For several years the second grade classes put on a 7 year old version of a three ring circus as a part of their social studies unit on community demonstrating the way people worked together. The chickens were always the stars. The kids wore the chickens on their heads, had them pop up out of hats, trained them to slide down slides, etc. We adults were always impressed with what the children had trained the chickens to do and how tame they had become. Interestingly, though the children were in no way intimidated by the chickens, none would ever agree to cook or eat the eggs saying, "You can't eat those eggs."

One afternoon I received a call from a neighbor who did not have children in our school. She excitedly stated, "I have a turkey in my front yard, is it yours?" It was not. Yet another day after the close of school a gentleman came into the office dragging a goat with a rope around its neck. He said, "I found it on Elmwood Drive, and I knew it was yours so I just brought it over here." It was not ours, and we had never seen it before. We did relieve him of his charge and learned that a private school several blocks from our school had animals and the goat belonged to them.

We were most fortunate to have Nancy Reagan, wife of President Ronald Reagan, visit our school as a part of her "Just Say No" initiative. My office was to be the site of a news conference so everything was tidied and the blinds and curtains pulled tightly closed as no one wanted the First Lady to see a courtyard that just might be somewhat dirty. As the conference progressed, the rooster crowed and Mrs. Reagan's immediate reaction was, "Did I hear a rooster crow?" One of those conducting the conference explained that we had chickens in the courtyard on the other side of the window. Mrs. Reagan was adamant that she wanted to see our chickens, so at the end of the conference we all trudged to the large windows overlooking the courtyard and Mrs. Reagan enjoyed our chickens.

A stray cat wandered in one day and made himself quite at home. After several days of having a persistent kitty visit the building, one of our secretaries took him home at night. After several visits to the vet to get his proper shots, the cat became known as Cameron and would come to school during the day, flop down in the office, and go with the secretary at night.

In the mid 90's the school was about to undergo an extensive renovation. I do not think my boss was ever particularly fond of the animals, but as we approached the renovation, he said to me one day, "It looks like you are going to keep those animals, so when the school is renovated, let's at least make a nice place (meaning neat and tidy) for them." Several teachers met with the architect and designed a simple barn with a concrete floor that could be easily cleaned. The courtyard was also divided into two sections, a place for the animals, and a place to watch and enjoy them.

The renovation, a nice barn with concrete floor and a place to watch the animals, opened up new opportunities for us. We added goats to our barnyard. Our first goat was a pregnant mother who soon after she arrived gave birth to two kids which we raised. Since, we have kept the goats, usually two, about a year, sent them to the farm in the summer and started again with babies in the fall. This year the baby goats arrived the first day of school with all of the children outside to greet the new "kids".

At one point following the renovation a well-meaning parent purchased a potbellied pig for the school, brought it in, chased around the building looking for me and attempted to present this "gift" wrapped in a blanket very proudly. My thinking was, "Why in the world would you do this without first asking the school if we wanted or could even keep a potbellied pig." I refused firmly but with kindness. I understand that the pig ended up being the household pet of one of her neighbors. Better the neighbor than us! That was only one of a number of situations where we were offered far more than we desired. In refusing similar "gifts," one has to be careful not to offend as these are the same families you are looking to for support in other situations.

Our "Courtyard Crew" was made up of students in grades 3-6 who liked to come in early in the morning to feed and clean. I was often surprised by the children who volunteered as they were often not the ones you thought would be anxious or willing to get dirty. Under the supervision of a staff member, the "Courtyard Crew" brought a pair of old shoes on the first day of school which they put on and out they went before school, in their uniforms to greet, feed and clean the animals. Courtyard duties included not only watering and feeding but scooping up the soiled hay and disposing of it, hosing the area down so it did not smell and of course offering a generous amount of love daily.

It was not just the goats that were the hit with the kids. They loved the chickens just as much. Each one was named by the students. We had to thin our flock once or twice a year as we had new chicks hatching in both fall and spring. One of our county construction crew had a farm just south of our area and was always anxious and/or willing to take the ones we decided to send. Thinning the flock was often traumatic as the children never wanted to give any of them up and you frequently heard, "You can't take that one, it's my favorite." Most of our chickens were hatched and raised in our courtyard. When we began, to get some variety of breeds, we annually ordered a sampling of various bantam breeds from a hatchery in the Midwest.

The courtyard was not just fun; it developed responsibility in those caring for the animals. As explained to the students each fall, the animals could not feed and water themselves. They were completely dependent upon the kids to take care of them every day. Melissa, age 9, commented "I like to help clean and it makes me feel better to know they are taken care of. It's taught me to be more responsible." The preschoolers in our day care center, ages 2 and up, visited the courtyard at least once every day. If you asked the youngest of them what those feathered animals were, they quickly exclaimed "chicks."

We were often teased and called "The Animal School" which was not offensive to us. When I greeted former students regardless of their age, the first question always asked of me was, "Do you still go camping, do you still go to Williamsburg and do you still have the animals?" The animals created some wonderful and lasting memories for all of us.

What I learned:

- Kids (children) and animals belong together.
- Don't try to thin your flock when students are around the courtyard.
- Children happily clean animal refuse at school, yet most would not touch the stuff at home.
- Don't give "live" gifts to folks without asking and if you are on the receiving end refuse firmly but graciously.

"Touch the Screen Here, Mrs. Wilson"

Technology has not only changed the way we live, it has changed the way we work with students and manage schools. In the 1970's we were thrilled to receive our first electric typewriter, an IBM Selectric. The Selectric allowed us to change the font, correct typos and do everything much more quickly, easily and accurately then it had ever been done previously. Imagine several years later when we received our first computer.

Our first IMB computer arrived in a fancy off white laminate case which we placed proudly in the front office. As we had no real idea what to do with it, we simply made certain that everyone who came in knew that we had one. After sitting for several months, we slowly learned how to record attendance and maintain student and staff information. For routine office work, we still relied on the IBM Selectric. Today, tasks in the school office would not even be attempted without a computer as that would be almost foolish.

For the last several years, it seemed the school office was ruled by emails which were both a blessing and a curse. It was not uncommon for a principal to receive between seventy-five and a hundred a day. Of course parents and teachers expected an almost immediate reply which was sometimes difficult or impossible. With our "Blackberry's" we were indeed accessible to the world twenty-four hours a day. All of our reports, plans, report cards, and information were done using the computer.

Each school day began with a live broadcast of the Cameron School News on closed circuit television broadcast throughout the building. Youngsters were trained to write the script and ably set up and operate all of the equipment including cameras, lighting, sound, and monitors. Following the Pledge of Allegiance, Cameron School Song and the "Moment of Silence," birthdays were announced, presentations awarded, students recognized, and of course the lunch menu read. Our third through sixth grade newscasters, under the supervision of the librarian, began the school every day with excitement, creativity and enthusiasm sharing the specialness of the day, ethnic holidays and celebrations. The news concluded with students reciting the Cameron School Pledge which follows:

Cameron School Pledge

"We the students of Cameron Elementary School
Pledge to be the best that we can be
We will respect ourselves, adults and our peers.
We will come to school with an open mind
Ready to accept the challenges of the day.
We will bring in our homework

and work hard to complete it with excellence.
This is our pledge of honesty, trust and obedience
I pledge that I will accept the consequences of my own actions by
not blaming others for the decisions I make."

Written by Dr. Lillie M. Hill Vinson, teacher

It took a while before computer use trickled down to the classroom level. Now, teachers are issued an up to date laptop on their first day of employment. Beyond that, technology has permeated every phase of instruction in the classroom. In the last two or three years as I entered classrooms to observe, I realized that what we could do with technology for students was almost beyond my comprehension. We could teach a lesson using an interactive Smart Board, pull a video off the internet into the middle of the lesson to further explain what was being taught only to return to the Smart Board and complete the lesson. A teacher could do this at almost any time and for any subject while the students were directly engaged with a "hands on" process. The days of sitting and listening to the teacher talk were over.

Learning to use technology for instruction proved a challenge for many teachers. Though they were excellent teachers, they were reluctant to accept change and keep up with the times. It was embarrassing for them to realize that their children knew and understood the programs they wanted to use better than they did. I remember observing a first grade math lesson with a more experienced teacher just learning to use the Smart Board. In spite of her efforts, the Smart Board just would not do what she wanted it to. Finally, Marvin, one of the first graders, politely got up without being told, went to the board, touched the screen and announced, "Touch the screen here, Mrs. Wilson." The teacher thanked Marvin and the lesson progressed. Regardless of how effective you might have been as a teacher, if you hadn't kept up with the changes as they occurred, your effectiveness was gradually diminished.

It was so much fun to watch the kindergarten students interact with the Smart Board. Their teacher, Mrs. David, was a master. From day one the five year olds began to learn letters, letter sounds, matching and basic math. Within days they became experts. It was almost funny to watch kindergarten students try to teach a substitute how to use the Smart Board. The poor substitute was intimidated by youngsters at age 5 trying to teach them how to do their job. On more than one occasion I had kindergarten students come to me and say, "Mr. or Mrs. ...., they don't know anything."

As older elementary students sat in class, each with their own laptop provided and loaned them by the school, opportunities with technology were thus made available to every child regardless of home background or family finances. Students were so proud of their personal laptops, guarding and handling them with great care. It became immediately obvious from the moment they were first issued, that these "netbooks" were a "dream come true" for most of our kids. They named them, checked on them, took them to lunch with them and only let them out of their sight when absolutely necessary.

Students interacted globally with other students as well as those within the school. Students, individually or as a team, planned, researched and developed their own programs,

"Power Points" or presentations. The student driven competition was fierce as each strived to be as creative as possible making certain that theirs was better than those of anyone else. Students learned from each other, taught each other, encouraged each other and praised each other. It was amazing what they had learned to do.

Some elementary students were computer experts to the extent that we called upon them to diagnose, analyze or repair problems. Alfredo, the smartest elementary computer geek I have ever known, could actually make a computer and spoke a language most of us adults didn't very often understand. He conversed with our school system technology department as he spoke on the level of the experts. Alfredo was also the driving force behind the morning closed circuit television show, able to make our system work and perform tasks that we could only have dreamed about.

While some students were amazing with their computer knowledge, there were dangers as they often had the knowledge to do more than they were lawfully or legally allowed to do. Technology also had its dangers in schools and required us to constantly monitor for inappropriate websites which seemed to pop up more quickly than we could identify them. When students used the library or worked independently on projects, which was at times very appropriate, the opportunity to stray away from the assignment existed. Not surprisingly, it was the boys who most often sought the inappropriate sites. As many of our children did not have access to the internet or to computers at home, school was the only place they could complete projects or assignments.

Cell phones were also a blessing and a curse in school. Mary got angry with Mrs. Jackson because she would not accept messy and incomplete homework. Mary went to the restroom, called mom on her cell phone crying about how awful Mrs. Jackson was. Mom's response was to come to the school in the middle of the school day, go to the classroom and verbally attack the teacher in front of the students. Mrs. Jackson was a highly regarded teacher. The students were angry with Mary for her actions. Mother was embarrassed as indeed the work was very poorly done. The situation benefited no one yet similar situations were repeated more than once. I understood why some parents wanted their children to have a phone which was fine as long as it was kept quiet and put away during the school day. Even with the teacher circulating, a child could still sit at his/her desk and discretely text other students, thus missing necessary instruction.

We suspected Shawn's mother was dealing drugs yet she gave Shawn the phone to take to school. No one suspected her involvement if a ten year old had the phone. Calls were left for mom during the day and when Shawn got home from school mother would retrieve them. On one occasion, the phone went off during the school day. The teacher took the phone, which we were allowed to do if they were not kept quiet. The parent was instantly ready to attack the school and everyone in it to get the phone returned to her.

Many phones contained cameras so pictures were taken or brief videos filmed. Roger was in the bathroom tearing it up, throwing toilet paper everywhere and making as big a mess as he could. When we discovered the mess and suspected the culprit, a "friend" was quick to tell us that Roger's friend Sam had videoed the entire incident. The evidence was all there. The phone was not returned to school. Roger cleaned up the mess. Roger also got his act together.

Technology will no doubt continue to invade schools as it has our lives in ways we can hardly imagine today. I envision schools without textbooks in the not too distant future as almost everything today can be accessed using the internet. The ultimate benefit of all of this technology will depend entirely on how it is used to promote learning.

What I learned:

- **The uses of technology for instruction are almost unimaginable.**
- **Teachers must keep current with technology.**
- **If you are doing something you shouldn't be, don't let your friends video it.**
- **Many students know more than their teachers about technology.**

Resilient Kids/Fragile Kids

As being a "kid" in our modern day becomes ever more difficult, children face many increasing demands. Academic demands, social (clothing) demands, and the demands of sports are just a few. In today's world for children, we add individual characterizations, often critical, on the social networks of Facebook, My Space, etc. The list is exhaustive. Children from poverty face even greater risks because they are entering the picture with little in terms of financial support. Their need for approval and acceptance by others, both peers and adults is critical.

Ricardo was a fourth grader born in Honduras and arriving in the United States at age three. Ricardo's family consisted of mother, younger brother and sister and a newborn. Very devoted to her children, Mother floated from job to job working periodically at a variety of local ethnic restaurants. The family, as a result, had only meager financial resources. Ricardo moved from school to school since kindergarten and from shared apartment to shared apartment often arriving home from school only to learn that the family was moving or had moved again. His bed was wherever he slept that particular night. Thanks to the McKinney-Vento Homeless Act we were fortunate to be able to keep Ricardo and his family in our school for more than two years. Thus, the children had a stable school environment.

Every adult in our school knew and loved Ricardo. He was a good student, hard working, and always prepared. Ricardo tried to please, completed his school work and had an ever present smile on his face. His positive attitude consistently won him the respect of adults. Ricardo was always kind, setting an example of good character because "Character Counts at Cameron" and appreciative of everything that was done for him.

On a field trip to the State Capitol building and State Fair, Ricardo, who had no "spending money" from his family, looked down as we toured in the State Capitol and picked up a $ 100 dollar bill that was laying on the floor. None of the other students or adults had seen it. Not surprising, Ricardo immediately signaled the tour guide and turned the bill over to him. The tour guide took Ricardo's name and the address of the school. Happily, several weeks later, Ricardo received a check for $ 100 from the State Capitol expressing their appreciation for his honesty and indicating that no one had claimed or sought the money, so it was being returned to him. Ricardo became our hero.

Rebecca was a fifth grader who lived with her two older sisters and an aunt. Early on mother was out of the picture and custody given to their hard working father. He had a wonderful sense of humor as he doted on the three girls and did his best to provide both a loving and stable home and family environment for his children. Father was stricken with cancer and died when Rebecca was in third grade. Custody was transferred to an aunt who has since devoted her life to raising the three girls with the support of other family members and the church that they attend.

Rebecca struggled as a student and had to work to keep up with the class. She was usually successful. Her aunt constantly monitored Rebecca's progress and remained in contact weekly with the teachers offering whatever academic support she could. The aunt made certain that Rebecca was able to take advantage of tutoring, Saturday School and remedial opportunities that were available and would promote Rebecca's academic standing. The aunt also worked outside of the school to make every possible learning experience available that the family could afford and expected the best from all three girls. Always neat and in school uniform, Rebecca was a happy child, always spoke and maintained wonderful relationships with peers and staff. She was eager to please and knew she was loved and accepted as a part of our school.

Senior was a small, handsome second grader. Senior lived with mother, father and a younger brother not yet in school. Mother cleaned houses, and father was a laborer. Neither parent spoke much English, nor had more than limited formal educations. They lived in the tiny basement apartment of a small duplex home. Though you never saw mom and dad or heard from them in school, you were quick to realize that appreciation for education had been taught at home as Senior took every academic task seriously and was successful at school. Senior was eager to demonstrate his academic skills and though he was reserved and quiet, his hand was always the first to go up whenever a question was asked. His answer was most often right on target and you could easily feel and share in his pride. He loved math, learned it easily, and often achieved beyond his classmates. His level of motivation and classroom behavior was what every teacher desires in every student every day.

Senior was at the top of his second grade level academically and was always well prepared for school which he took very seriously. In spite of limited finances, the support, encouragement and expectation of family was obvious as Senior arrived daily with supplies, homework and in a sparkling white shirt and navy blue slacks. He looked like a young professor in his glasses which you never saw him without. Senior's attitude could only be described as "the best." Every day he won the hearts of the adults as he came to school eager to learn. An excellent citizen, though certainly not a sissy, Senior sought to please adults and maintain positive relationships with peers. You could feel his annoyance when classmates misbehaved or wasted learning time in the classroom.

Miriam was a fourth grader who needed lots of love, approval and reassurance. Miriam loved to talk about her family and lived in one room with her mom and dad, third grade brother, and two preschool sisters in a small house that the family shared with a number of unrelated adults. Dad seemed to have limited work. Mom cleaned rooms at a local hotel. Though Miriam had been at Cameron since kindergarten, none of the staff had ever met or seen either parent. Miriam was an attractive and happy child who never complained but liked to cling and hug any adult that was close by. She sought constant positive reinforcement and acceptance from the adults who were present.

Miriam struggled academically though she received additional support from the ESOL teacher daily. She seemed aware of her academic struggle and knew that others around her were mastering the subject matter more easily than she. Though her behavior and attitude were flawless, preparedness for school was inconsistent with homework being completed only some of the time. The staff provided all of the basic school supplies for Miriam and her brother and paid for field trips so that they could participate with the other students. Watching Miriam and her brother, it was clear that both the school breakfast and lunch were heavily relied upon as part of the basic diet. She would frequently tell you how delicious the school food was and what her favorites were. Miriam and her brother never had any money for ice cream or any kind of a treat at lunch. Miriam was always clean and well cared for, but her clothes were worn for at least several days and were often too small.

Isaiah arrived at Cameron at the end of fourth grade very much out of place with inappropriate clothes, a wild hairdo and looking like a little thug. Several days following his arrival, the teacher came to me and reported that Isaiah was extremely smart and was an excellent student. Shortly thereafter, in my first real conversation with Isaiah, I remarked that I was sure he missed his friends from his other school. He replied that he did not have any friends because he had never been in any school long enough to make any friends. He went on to say that he moved about every three months.

Isaiah, currently a sixth grader, shared a house with his mother, kindergarten sister and an unrelated family. Fortunately, mother has been able to remain in this house for more than a year and told me several times that Cameron had been a real "blessing" for Isaiah because he had good friends, liked school and was doing well academically. He was in an accelerated learning program working at least a year above grade level in all subjects.

You immediately recognized from conversation that Isaiah was happy in school. He appeared one day proud of his new and more traditional hair cut though no one had ever said anything about his hair. Isaiah's teachers, however, recognized his academic talents and abilities and praised, encouraged and complimented him routinely on his daily school performance. By the end of fourth grade Isaiah was asking questions of the teachers and helping other students. He was eager to tell you that Mr. Sachs, his teacher, said he was smart and that he expected to make Honor Roll this grading period. Isaiah's success led to further successes, and we were very proud of his academic achievement. Thank goodness Mr. Sachs was able to look beyond initial appearances.

Veronica shared the family home with her mom who worked at the post office and was a former Cameron student. Dad was in and out of the picture until an untimely and questionable death when Veronica was in first grade. Though dad did not live with Veronica and her mom at that time, his death was very traumatic for her, and she stopped growing academically and seemed to lose interest in everything including school. Since the death of her father, with the support of the classrooom teachers and special education staff, Veronica again became interested in school and in time daily appeared to be a very happy child.

The additional academic support Veronica received in a small classroom setting enabled her to more easily establish positive relationships with teachers and students who were experiencing the same learning difficulties that she was. Though she continued to struggle to get on grade level, she made steady progress. With the continued support of capable teachers and her mother, she will continue to grow academically to become a successful adult.

Unlike children from more middle class and affluent surroundings, the teacher's praise and acceptance was paramount to the school success of children from poverty. Relationships, relationships, relationships!! Whether or not the teacher "likes me" was often the difference between success and failure. Kids did not do their best for the teachers who they perceived did not like them, whether or not that was true. Because a child knew he/she was liked and appreciated by the teacher did not mean that they would always behave because that may not have been the case at all. The feeling of acceptance and student classroom behavior shouldn't be combined. Children often believed that the teacher liked those kids who were well behaved and did not like those who were not. And, there was an element of truth to that. Bob recently asked me to call Ms. Jackson, his teacher from the last school year who had retired and tell her he missed her. Though Bob's behavior and work habits routinely brought him into conflict with Ms. Jackson, he knew that he was liked by her. His comment, "This new teacher, I know she don't like me much."

Children from middle class backgrounds had the support of parents at home, knew that they were expected to do well in school, and knew that they would receive support if they could not achieve. Many of our children and our parents were far more dependent on us for academic success.

Our fifth grade team of teachers was an example of those who routinely modeled acceptance. When children arrived with all of their issues, academic, behavioral and social, they were simply welcomed for who they were. Some of these children had come close to residing in the office in past years because of poor behavior, but once in fifth grade, their name was never again uttered in a negative light. When a new child enrolled or a child from the Alternative Education class was ready to be mainstreamed, they simply said, "Send them on." These teachers knew their subject matter and taught it well. However, their best quality was that they simply accepted kids and treated them like they were worthy of that acceptance.

Kids knew who was real and who was phony, who liked them and who didn't. Kids forgave us when we did not teach at our best. However, they had difficulty forgetting those they perceived did not "like them." Kids did not enter a new classroom each fall seeking to be accepted by changing to meet the need of a particular teacher. Children entered a new classroom each fall hoping to be accepted for who they were, and based on that acceptance, became motivated to change and improve themselves. The ability to accept all children regardless of background, behavior and social issues, and treat each with care was a special quality not possessed by everyone.

What I learned:

- **Many children from backgrounds of poverty struggle simply to survive every day and achieve in spite of their circumstances.**
- **School is far more than an academic institution to many children.**

- Children from poverty who excel and the teachers who teach, love and accept them are indeed heroes in their own right.
- Exceptional teachers know their subject matter and establish nurturing and caring relationships with every child in their care regardless of background.

Everybody's Favorite Teacher

Every adult or older child can look back on his or her own life and recall certain truly outstanding teachers who made a profound and lasting impact on them. Those teachers were a combination of young and old, men and women, different ethnicities, etc. However, each of those teachers was outstanding to their students for a different reason. Teachers were and still are the heartbeat of the school. If youngsters learned it was because of what their teachers planned, organized, taught, explained and modeled in individual classrooms. If youngsters didn't learn, the fault also fell upon the teachers. As principal, the most critical part of my job was to make certain that every child at every grade had the most highly trained, competent and capable teachers. It was also my job to see that those teachers had the resources needed to successfully do their important job.

My experience in schools carried me into the classrooms of the very best and others I would not recommend. In Mrs. Compton's first grade you quickly began to learn responsibility and develop character when she said, "Thank you, Todd, for remembering to push your chair in," and every chair in the class got pushed in. "I like the way Susan is sitting quietly doing her work," and every child got to work right away. "We have a guest," and all sat up straight. We called it "Positive Reinforcement." Those few "Thank you's" or "I like the way's" made a lasting impact as children grew and developed into respectful, thoughtful students and citizens. With Mrs. Compton's kind voice, statements like those brought order, calm and understanding into the class creating situations where children knew they were appreciated, respected and what was expected of them in terms of their achievement. Meaningful sayings like, "Remember, always be happy for the other person," went a long way when Amy won but Maria did not and thought she should have. Such language served to remind children that each would have a turn, each would win or be first at some time and, each was special.

One could never forget Mr. Hampton's sixth grade math class. Unlike many upper elementary teachers who struggle with ever more complicated math, he understood math inside and out. It made sense to him. One of his great teaching strengths was that he was able to convey that "making sense" to others. Many times I heard from former students, "Seventh grade math was easy, I was in Mr. Hampton's math class," or a child in confusion told by a classmate, "He/She needs to be in Mr. Hampton's math class." Children readily forgave our weaknesses, but they respected knowledge, individual teacher strengths, and knew quickly whether or not you really understood what you were teaching. Not only did Mr. Hampton teach math to many of our older students, he tutored countless ones who needed extra help and support before or after school. Mr. Hampton expected each student to behave, do his homework and know that he would really talk with your parents if you were having trouble. Every child understood, respected and appreciated those expectations. In Mr. Hampton's math class students were there to learn math and had a lot of fun doing it.

Every day in physical education class Mr. Stevens taught character, not just PE. He consistently had wise sayings that students quickly learned like, "Exercising will help you get smart," always preceded by "What does Mr. Stevens say?" The children answered back to him as they had taken it all in. Mr. Stevens freely talked about his own family, growing up in the circus, the difficulty he had in school because he was and still is partially deaf. The constant message was, "If Mr. Stevens could do it, you can do it more easily because you are smarter than Mr. Stevens." Every class was told over and over that they were the smartest, best students he had ever taught. "Mr. Stevens is so proud of you." All children loved to be complimented, especially when it was sincere. The children always knew Mr. Stevens was sincere. As a juggler, Mr. Stevens met with older students before school on a weekly basis and taught the fundamentals of juggling. The activity was so popular that we were never able to include all of those that wanted to be included. More than physical education, Mr. Stevens communicated every day how much he cared about the students, how much he loved coming to school, how much he loved teaching PE and how much he appreciated their hard work. Do you suppose there was ever a discipline problem in Mr. Stevens' class? Of course there was not.

Every school year there was a small group of students and their families who were forced to deal with handicaps: Autism, learning disabilities, mental limitations, physical limitations, and health limitations. They were our most fragile kids, both academically and socially. Too often they were the students who teachers really preferred not to deal with in their classrooms. They were too much trouble, required too much attention, or needed too many academic accommodations outside of the norm. Yet, in Mrs. Croll's primary special education class you found a unique, loving and nurturing environment where every child was accepted to the point that the students did not themselves recognize that limitations existed. They all became "just kids." They were excited about school, excited about learning, yet very safe; protected by a caring, loving individual and several assistants who not only taught you but walked with you, ate lunch with you, read with you and held your hand if it needed to be held. Always fun to visit and always happy, the students were proudly anxious to share what they were learning and doing.

In Mr. V's sixth grade, the students quickly advised you that he not only taught them social studies, but taught them life as well. His life lessons as he shared openly with students, explained his struggles and trials as a high school and a college student, a teenager, an employee in a pizza shop, a kid who did not have a lot of extra money. His father was an elementary teacher, and he was a child with four siblings. Mr. V talked about the pitfalls of growing up, what to embrace, what to avoid and who to and who not to hang around with. He taught them what and how teachers think, and who they needed to impress and "get in their corner" in order to be most successful in school. Mr. V encouraged students to respect their families, help their parents and support their siblings. He shared the meaning of current events in their lives and taught them how to begin to plan for a career that would be meaningful and purposeful.

Mr. V explained that he was an average kid growing up, a typical teenager. He was able to pass on good advice to carefully listening adolescents. Lest it sound like this was the basis of his class, far from it. Students were always actively engaged with a variety of up- to-date and exciting interactive technology. Mr. V was always prepared, seldom sat at his desk instead stood in front of the class explaining, questioning, information giving. Students knew Mr. V as a seeking, learning teacher who formed respectful relationships that kids could hang on to as they went from elementary to middle school and beyond. Mr. V loved learning and related the events of the day to social studies and how and why students would be impacted by these daily happenings in the future. Social studies became relevant to students daily lives.

Every child wanted to be in Mrs. Rogers' class because, she cared, she was fun, she was exciting, she was herself a learner and she would engage you in your learning every day. To be sure, you would behave because Mrs. Rogers didn't play around. Yet annually in the spring, I received notes, lots of notes, from parents and children, asking that I made certain that their children were in her class the following year. More than occasionally parents greeted me at the Open House before the opening of school and begged for their children to be in her room. One parent said that his daughter had not slept a single night since she learned she was not assigned to Mrs. Rogers. Mrs. Rogers' magic? As Julia put it, "She teaches from the heart, and we know she loves us every day even when we're bad." It was always the unconditional acceptance that made the difference. There was no substitute for the approval of the teacher regardless of who you were, what baggage you brought to school, what your behavioral history was or how academically talented you might or might not have been.

That youngsters do not like strict teachers was an absolute myth. Students desired teachers who had control and made them behave. Many of our youngsters believed that we (teachers) were the ones who made them good, not that the goodness could come from within them. A visit to Mrs. Rogers' class consistently found her on her feet in front of the class, not at a desk. The summer found her preparing for fall and the opening of school. On a visit one saw active kids, happy kids, motivated kids, working and learning. Mrs. Rogers was the motivator and numerous academic success stories existed because of her.

One did not have to be a classroom teacher to make an impact on student lives. Art, music, and physical education teachers not only provided learning opportunities, they developed and recognized talents and skills in youngsters that would carry them throughout their lives. Mrs. Jacobs treated every one of our 500+ children as though they were artists, saved a selection of each one's work, mounted displays of art work around the school and at the end of the school year transformed the building into a gigantic art gallery. What better way was there to tell every child they were worthy, special, and they had unique strengths? Mrs. Jacobs' Art Show was like an opening on Broadway. All of the students were involved helping get the school ready. They walked around admiring their art as the night came together. On the night of the big show everyone dressed up for the evening and walked down the red carpet into an atmosphere of creativity, beauty and pure joy to show their parents and guests what a wonderful job they had done. There were smiles, hugs and lots of laughter. Students were individually videoed giving their remarks and opinions about an evening that no one would soon forget.

Students were greeted and treated like college students in Mr. Northrop's math class. Mr. Northrop taught math every day at a high level expecting that each child was capable of learning any material or concept that he presented. End-of-year test scores consistently proved that to be true. What was the difference? The difference was his expectation of each child's ability to learn. As Mr. Northrop approached the children, it was with the deeply ingrained belief that he was capable of instructing you and that you were capable of learning whatever he taught. Unfortunately, some really hard working, caring teachers simply have not held fast to that belief. As a result, some gave up on kids too easily, accepted less than quality work or taught at a simpler level because they believed it was the best the children could do.

These were but a very few of the scores and scores of outstanding teachers with whom I worked. Each with different strengths, each was an individual and each special in his or her own right. They were mothers, fathers, care givers, nurses, and missionaries. They were ordinary folks who did extraordinary things for kids to make certain that they learned and had opportunities to grow and become happy productive and caring citizens. School was not work or a job to them. School was helping kids learn and be proud of themselves. School was where these teachers were found every day because they liked it there. They impacted the "Quality of the Future" every day.

What I learned:

- Teachers come in all shapes, sizes, genders, qualities and ages that make them special to kids.
- To be the best, teachers must be able to "connect" with kids, know their subject well and care deeply.
- There are many teachers who are truly outstanding, not just a few.
- Teaching is still the best thing you can ever do with your life.

Cameron School

Cameron School continues to be unique. The same is true for every school and every community. Once through the front door you encounter scores of smiling, happy faces in all hues and colors dressed in "Character Counts at Cameron" shirts or red and navy uniforms. There is much laughter, much hope, and much excitement about learning. A few steps beyond the door you find a courtyard with two tiny goats, and an assortment of chickens and rabbits. Several third and fourth grade student caretakers are carefully cleaning and feeding. On Wednesday morning before the school day begins you hear the joyous sounds of children throughout the building practicing as a part of two choirs. In the gym, jump rope and juggling are engaging youngsters in physical activity, and chess is being played in the cafeteria. Sixth grade boys and girls are dressed in their best for Girl Power and Boys Leadership after school. Lessons to be learned for the day include not only reading, writing and arithmetic but character, citizenship, and cooperation as well.

Our "track record" with test scores continues to be excellent.

We consistently pass or exceed our state and school system goals and the Federal, "Annual Yearly Progress (AYP)," which is a credit to the dedicated staff. Student accomplishments extend far beyond the test. In classrooms technology is apparent with Smart Boards and lap tops engaging students in the most active forms of learning. Teachers use digital cameras as we used paper and pencil. Pictures and videos of student activities are recorded. Classroom websites are anxiously shared with anyone who desires to view them. It is truly an exciting place to go to school and an exciting time to be a teacher or a student.

My lessons as principal have left me full of joy and hope for our future as a global society. Kids continue to be spontaneous, caring and appreciative of the opportunities made available to them just as they were forty years ago. I sometimes wonder if they learned as much as I.

Upon becoming principal I never thought that I would supervise the multi-million dollar renovation of a large building, deal with escaped prisoners, offer travel directions, worry about the safety of our children as the DC sniper was shooting around the beltway or walk the halls during a tornado threat making certain that little heads were down. I have taught countless classes, cleaned up many messes, put on Band-Aids and made several annual emergency trips to the hospital with those sick or injured. I have attended numerous weddings, birthdays and graduations, buried at least four and delivered several eulogies. I have been accepted as a part of different cultures and learned about Eid, Ramadan, the Chinese New Year, Cinco de Mayo and other ethnic celebrations.

I continue to ask myself the question, "If our kids can develop outstanding relationships with each other regardless of background, birthplace, language or skin color, why can't we adults be taught to do the same?" Love, kindness and caring are never out of style and coupled with excellent, compassionate and enthusiastic teachers lay the groundwork for what is to come not only for our Nation but for the entire world.

Through my forty years I have continually been inspired by the following quote from Carl Sandburg:

REMEMBRANCE ROCK

"SOME SACRED SEED LURKS IN EACH HUMAN PERSONALITY NO MATTER HOW LOWLY ITS ARRIVAL ON EARTH. TO GIVE EVERY SUCH SEED THE DEEPEST POSSIBLE ROOTS AND THE HIGHEST POSSIBLE FLOWERING IS IN THE VISION AND HOPE OF THOSE IDEAS OF FREEDOM AND DISCIPLINE WHICH CONSTITUTE THE AMERICAN DREAM."

CARL SANDBURG

To give every child regardless of his or her origin or circumstance the deepest roots and the highest flowering is the job of teachers and principals who daily mold the future. The son of a fireman, the first one in my family to go to college, I have and continue to live the American Dream thanks to those teachers who struggled, encouraged and cared for me. May I be an inspiration to others who seek to meet the rewards and challenges of managing a school and school community.

Appendix 1

"Teacher, Please Excess Jane"

Every school receives dozens of excuses, some truthful, some not, many poorly written. Some of the examples saved follow. They are printed as received without corrections:

"Excuse Maria from school 5/26-5/28. She has been experiencing major Mechanical malfunctions brought about by her fathers car. Please send home the necessary work for Maria to pass. Thank you"

"To Whom It May Concern. If you get sick put him in a sink with hot water run in the sink, and put a towel on his head. If that donot help in a hour call me at work, Maria Smithway, 703 712 0912 and say Number #38"

"Steven was out because of death Mrs. Susan Flowers"

"Dear Mrs. Creek and Mrs. Hines I apologize for Chris' tardiness.

Our alarm clock failed to go off and we are all running late. Sincerely, Laurie Mendoza"

"Dear Mrs. Creamer or to whom it may concern Antoinette's nee. Antoinette has injured her right nee. Was struck by a base-ball bat. Mrs. Daniel Simpson"

"Dear Mrs. Sasha, Susan has been with the chicken since Jan 21-23. She may come back tomorow I'm not sure. Jackie White"

"Please excuse Thomas for being absent on Wesnday & Turday of last week, I had labor on Wesnday and delivered my new Son on Turday night. Mrs. Coffey (Mother)"

"Teacher, Please excess Jane yesterday for missing school. We went out of town and did not get back in time for her to go too school, Mrs Jones"

"Mrs. Cline I am sorry Eddy has miss this time from school but he has really been sick he's been in and out of hospital for different test so please Keep an Eye on him If you notice anything funny about him Like he falls over his own feet or anything please write me a note and let me no. Please send work home with him. Thanks Nancy King"

"Dear Mrs. McMillan Bobbie Jo was in the hospital for tests and exrays yesterday. I sill don't know anything. She is on a muscle relaxer for her stomach right now. If she gets sick send her home, But I will be at school at 2:30 to see the play by Mrs. Smith's class.

Something has happened with the boys flipping up skirts and some boy flipped hers and teased her about what he saw and she's gotten so modest and secretive about her body in the last month. She won't let the doctors look where they need to. I've had my hands full with her.

Her papers are done. If she needs more to catch up-please send them home. Mrs. Carolyn Meredith"

"Leonard will not be in school because we think he has accumulated the measles"

"Ruth is sick and Mary is mental. I have a hard time to control with Mary. If she is saying she is sick in school teacher will have to control her."

"Please excuess Danielle's absence from school yesterday. She was kindly of sick. Thank you Mrs. Collins"

"Ricky was late. We had a "clothes" discussion. Lorie Johnson"

"Veronica has not been going to school because she had fevers, headaches and a sore throat. Sometimes Veronica cannot or would not eat a lot. Leonardo Vasquez"

"Jeremy is late because the cat stepped on the alarm clock and turned it off"

"Mary has a problem with her mind. She was wild and her head hit on the wall She was also wild in the morning Could you see she go to Mental Health or doctor"

"Mrs. Curry:

There was an accident at our house yesterday; the cabinet fell off the wall and it hit Rebecca on the head and some dishes fell out and cut her leg. I don't want her running or jumping around or doing any ruff playing today.

Also I will be picking Rebecca up around 11:30 to go on a trip to her grandparents house today. Thank you! Amy Naylor"

"Why Henry was out of school we went to W Va because of my dad was sick Mrs. Akin"

"Mrs. Curry I want for Martha to come home of the bus at 12: 00 Because she has to go to the hospital Thank you Gladys Montenegro"

Mrs. Dillow, you have my permitten to take Joe to the eye clinik"

"Susie has spring her arm and I was going to keep her home but she wanted to come to school. Mrs. Banner"

"Mrs. Green- Miriam isn't going to school because she is sick. That is why she isn't going. Could you send her homework with Ana. Thank you Signed Victoria Gonzales"

"Dear Mrs. Fox

Carrie was sick with an upset stomach Tuesday evening and early Wednesday. She revived around lunch time and managed to drive her father into a state of pure nerves and the dog got so upset he nipped her. I can't put into words how happy they are that she is well enough to come back to school. Enjoy! Thank you Mrs. Ernest Fry

"Dear Mrs. Fox,

Please excuse angela at two o'clock Because my mom is coming to pick me up for a check-up and I need angela and I can't take the kids with me. She has to walk home and I would apresi-ate it if you would let her go for the Day. Please give her the Homework she will miss out on okay?" Mary Strick gaurdient"

"to:tommy teacher

tommy is not possible to atent to the school today because, he don't feel well. Maria Rodriguez"

"Ms Cleary

Missy was absent from school on Friday, because she had a sore throat and was croupy. So I keep her home, got her to gargle and gave her cough syrup. She's better. Mrs. Donna Dixon"

"To whom it may concern

Kevin, Ruthie and Duncan has been out sick with a cold and a 24hr flu bug which had them irregular so please don't think for a minute that they were kept home without an excuse

Also they do not have lunch money for today or tomorrow so if possible let them have lunch and I will pay what they owe on Monday Thank you Alice Coffman"

"Mrs Dearst Please excuese Ricky from been absent from school he has been very sick and he is still having trouble with his stomach thank you Betty Hoffman"

"Mrs. Krause

Please excuse CJ for being absent tuesday Mommy was ill and did not hear the alarm go off Mrs. McKee"

"Mrs. Dearst

I am sending note by Ricky the reason he hasn't been to school. I had to go away because of illnesses and I sent him up to his mother. I will see that he won't miss any more school. I am sorry this happen. Please forgive me. Thank you.. Sue Ann"

" Mrs. Bagley

Excuse Colleen Aikens from being absent yesterday. She was not ill. She had to go get new shoes. Mrs. Aikens"

"Juan was feeling too tired to go to school. Mrs. Juan Rodriguez"

"We over slep Marie Castle"

"Please excuse Charlies' absence as there has been a death in the family. I would have called but I broke my toe last night"

"I kept Leslie home today because she has something broke out all over her legs. And during the night some went to her back & chest. Has the chickenpox been going around at school? Mrs. Carroll

APPENDIX 1

"TO WHOM T MAY CONCERN. I Mrs. Maria Smithway is writing this letter for my son Edwood Arnold. He is a little ill this morning. So if you start feeling bader call me at work (Kmart 703 798-0304) and ask for Mrs. Charlene Smithway. But first talk to the manager and let him know that Edwood is ill and that I got to come get him. Because Edwood been ill for 3 days now.

PS Thank you and call me when you call me, at 10:30 AM Because sometime your job donot beleave when you say your child is ill so call me if Edwood donot get better"

"Dear Sir I want to say that only for tomorrow Meredith and Mary Ann have an appointment for nutrition, they will not come. From next day they will come regularly. Beside that I am sending you a copy of their immunisation card it may be necessary Thank you S Samidi"

"My son, James Coleman is late this morning-we had a discussion over whether or not he could wear new shoes 2 sizes too big for him. Sincerely, Julia Coleman"

"Jeffrey Smith will not be in school on Nov 16. He is attending his Mother's and Dad's wedding Mrs. Smith"

"Mrs. Tuck Anthony ain't feeling none to good. I was wanting him to stay home, but he wanted to come to school. So if you have any problem call me at work 571 251-5495. Have a good day Anna Ortega"

What I learned:

- Children who can't read, write and spell, grow up to become adults who can't read, write and spell.
- Many communications to the school are completed hastily.
- We pray we are able to teach our current students to be better able to write and spell than many of their parents.

Appendix 2

"The Key is in the Refrigerator on the Back Porch"

Notes and messages are received in schools countless times every day in writing, by phone, and increasingly by email. Some are serious, some are funny, some are poorly written and some just don't make any sense to those of us who receive them. The following are some that I thought were unique. They are printed as they were received.

Mrs. McDonald I am glad you are concern about Jimmy behavior. I am sorry how he behaved. He will not behave poorly on and other field trip that his class go on. Thank you very much Maria Smith I have seen Kenneth report cards and I miss place it

Dear mr. Tarly Leroy say that he did not say that and went Leroy say he did not do something he do not tell a lie that man that say that Leroy call him a hunky that is just kidding his mother will be out thay tomorrow THIS IS HIS FATHER

To whom it may concern David has my concent to be in course (chorus) Thank you Mary Britton

Melanie Harris do not have a phone so there is no way to call home. My nebighor Mrs. Allen is not home at all time doing the day-here is her number 703 913-**** Mrs. Allen do not be at home all day. My daughter is not able to walk down to the school to pick up Melanie we have only one car with three family and it has to be use for work. Could you please let us know what the trouble is Thank you Mr Ralph & Mrs Harris

Patrick will be picked up today by Betsy Gordon who is Mrs. Washburn's sister. Only for today-because Mrs. Washburn is doing something Thank you very much Martha Britton Patrick's Mother

Mrs. Bragg, I am giving Melissa permission to go on the field trip, but you should also know that Melissa can not swim, no matter what she says to impress her classmates, she can not swim, so please only allow her to be in the stand up area of the pool and wear a swim jacket. Thank you Mrs. Sharrod

To Mrs. Thomas from your well teached students and we wish you a Merry Christmas ands a happy new year.

End of day announcement over loudspeaker "Brian, the key is in the refrigerator on the back porch."

"Ricky, the key is under the door mat by the front door."

To whome it may Concern, I report to you that I am Nelda's

father and all my family is moving from Virginia to Maryland on May first

Nurse. I forgott my glasses again. Please save yourself the trouble and don't bother to get me. Love Diana

Dear Mrs. Atkinson

Today, Donald had alphabet letters from his kindergarten room in his desk. He also went into the other kindergarten room, took the class gerbil, put it in a small plastic bag and put it in his coat pocket.

Donald frequently helps himself to things that are not his. The occurrence with the gerbil seemed severe enough to me for you to be notified.

Would you please discuss this with Donald at home? Thank you for your help.

Sincerely yours, Mrs. Sara A. Wilson

To whom it may concern Our family has moved to another apartment and I was thinking if you are concerned about it: my new address is.....

I have gained custody of Marjorie and Toby Simpson for their best interest: due to the fact that they were living in a dangerous and unhealthy situation. There father had been repeatedly stabbed and in intensive care in the hospital and their mother had been arrested. Due to constant trouble in the home the social services were about to take the children when I went and picked them up. Everyone involved agreed that the children would be better off with me and my family. Maria Sorrell

(From a student) Dear Jennifer

I think you pretty and all. And I would go out with you but I go out with someone but me and that person is about to break up. You made my life different when I touched your soft hands

My number is 703 705-****

ps. I like you too

Love, Tommy

From a Student) Dear Mr. Towery Mrs. Brice wrote me up for no reason she say that I use bad words when I got off the bus, but she is the one who is using those bad words and the words she was saying is f, s, d and she blames me for things I never did. From Rodney Taylor

Mrs. Raymond It is alright for Daniela to go to the Tiny Tots concert. I would go but I have cramps, maybe next time. Thank you for wanting me to go with you. Mrs. Kingsley

Mr Rood Please excuse (Susie) for about 4 days the following week. We are taking a trip. Mrs. Nancy Castle

Mrs. White, Help-Ricky's friend tossed his book bag up onto the trailer outside of the school-my ladder was not long enough to reach-can one of the men at school help? Thank you- Lorie Robinson

Star didn't go to school last week because she was in Richmond with her mother I'm keeping her this week and sending her to school. And I didn't have any books on the capitals her Aunt Mrs Jones

Dear Teachers "It's Summertime" Do anybody like some tupperwares for the summer? Your Tupperware Lady Emily 703 426-1271

Dear Mr. Towery Ms Singletary said that I said a bad word. Mr Towery I didn't say a bad word Because if I would have said a bad word I would have already had said that I said a bad word. Even if I said a bad word it is because I was mad that I didn't get to eat my lunch in the cafe with all the other people . Ps. I'm So Sorry that miss Singletary said that I said a bad word. I will never lie to you Mr Towery Love Charlie Martin

Happy Birthday Mr. T I hope you have a nice Birthday. Finely your sweet 16 I don't know what to say, have fun, be good. Alls I whant to say is I hope your Birthday is a good one!

Mr. T your the best principal I've ever had and that's the truth if it wasn't I wouldn't be in school now. I think you're a person who some one can talk to you patient and very nice and that's something I Mark Martin should know! Lots of wishes! Mark M

Dear Mrs. Rush I have lost my patrol belt so I suppose I can't be a patrol wright. I'm sorry I can't be responsible if you want to chew me out by mail you can I'm prepared. I was hoping I could be a patrol until I went to middle school but I guess I can't. Well I will send you the money for the belt and badge when you send back the letter with the amount I have to pay give this note to Lisa and she will give it back to me.

Comments........

badge_____ Belt_____ Total + tax_____

Sincerely Carmella Quinton

To whom it may concern I want Tony to start writing his hold name Because it is something he do not know how to do. And plus he gets know sweets for two weeks or until his writing get better then it is and plus I'm not going to sign any of these work papers here until he start writing a hold sentence better then he do and I said for Tony to do all the words in back of the book. Okay to know the words you got to know how to spell write. But Tony said you want to know the words he not know how to spell and could you sen some math thing home with him. Because I donot know what typ of math you want him to do in addtion and subtraction. And plus I need some papers to put Tony in summer school Because he really need it. And by the way we are moving June 5 but Tony will still be with you until June 18 or 19. And if Tony ABC sentence not wrote over better then the one he got call me and I will come to school today but call me before 1:00 pm or make him do it before class start. Delores Johnson

Dear Mrs. Reed Chuck didn't finish his project Because he has been in the hospital this weekend his blood is real low again he might have to go back in there again this week we don't know yet. Maybe you can give him a few extra days on his project. Thank you Mrs. Mary Lou Ronson

Dear Mr. Donalson I apologize for Joey behavior I'm very shock to hear that he's been cutting up. My husband and I sat down and talked to Joe. I'm sure you won't have anymore problems with him. Thank you Mrs. Buckley

Dear Mr. Towery, It may seem a little strange getting a letter from a student who went there 7 years ago. Yes, it's been that long. I really can't believe it either. I felt that I had to write to you to let you know how I was doing. You try so hard to give us a good attitude about ourselves that I wanted to write about my accomplishments because of you. I can remember me being so insecure, but I guess we all are at that age. You helped us all, and I still see that you are leaving your care and love in other children as well. I read an article about you. To tell the truth, it made me swell with pride to say that I knew you. Well, to get on with it, I'm going to college here in Virginia. Either Longwood or Mary Washington. I can't wait to go! I plan to major in Political Science or French. I want to go into politics still. I remember when we had to write what we wanted to be when we grew up, and you wrote that story about our sixth grade class. I still want to be the first woman President. I still dream about that! I'm ready for the world, I just hope the world is ready for me!. I just want to tell you to keep up the good work, because you are doing a good job so far. God Bless You, Mary Allison

Mrs Daniels Kathy starting today must caught the 469 bus home from school this will bring her right home Thank you (Mother)

Dear Mr T, We went to the Smithsonian. First we went on the bus to the airport then we went to the subway station. We got are tickets on the subway. Everyone ate and then we went into the Smithsonian and saw lots of stuff like the presidents jacket and a very, very old school house! + when you look below there was the first cabin after that we went back on the subway and everything and we got back to the school. By Susan

Please Put Fred, if Eny Paper to Be sign Please Send them By him George

Dear Mr. Towery, We hope you could but you couldn't because you were busy. And in case you want to know where we went we went to the Smithsonian Museum. And it's a big place. And you should of saw the dinosaur it was in a glass window. There was big ones and little ones. Your friend Susan Whitman

Isaiah has been out of school for the last 7 days. And that is because of family problems. But I will be up there after I get home from work to talk about that. He need someone to show him his class. Thank You Ms. Collins

(From a Student) Dear Paul, Did you write that letter? If you did you are one nasty boy? I do not want a dollar cause it ain't going to be two minutes. Chrissy wants to know your answer (yes or no) Love, Lakeisha

(The following written message was received as a form of registration to enroll the child in school for the first time. Parent never came in.) This boy is my son his name is Samuel Smith Junior I am Samuel E Smith. He lives at 6732 Creekview Court Alexandria Va 92303 Telephone # 703 485 **** or 703 369 **** he will be riding the bus with Marissa James till when I can't say yet Sincerely yours Samuel E Smith

Mr. Towery I would like to say… I tried to think of something but my mind has just gone flat. So I'll just say, you're the type of leader I'd like to be someday. From Leslie Sowder

You shud been there. We had fun on the subway. It was difficult fore the tickets. Sometimes you had troubl. We had lunch in the rain. In the subway it was dark. When the lights go to on it is brignt. Sorry for my writinhand beaues we was on the subway. By TJ

Our class went to the Smithsonian. We saw a canon and sum of the things. There were guns and a sword and a picture of George Washington. From Jimmy

Dear Mrs Crimm Why Emily post card only have the time she was absent it don't have no check marks what kind of post card is this. So I am sending it back when you put marks on it I will sign it Sign Mrs Freeman

Miss Rush I will pick up Jackie's school pitchures up Wednesday when I get my check. I couldn't find any one to lend me any money Miss Handley

I am sorry I wont be able to come for pot lunch. I am and Susie are both is getting the flue. But if we get better in the next couple of days we will be there Thank you Betty A Mitchell

This is a notation that James and Edward to ride the bus until the end of the year. They will be Riding in the morning only but Theodore is to ride there and back. Thank you Ms Simmons

Wow, Mr. Towery! It is so neat to see you on Facebook. It seems like yesterday that you caught me in action, throwing toilet paper on the bathroom ceiling....then getting paddled by you in your office and that green vinyl couch sticks on my mind. What memories. I have to tell you, I learned a lot, had nothing but respect for you, and great memories of Lorton Elementary. I am the father of 3 kids and 2 Step-children, still live near my parents, and only wish my kids could have had experiences in elementary school like I did. You probably have left great marks on many peoples lives. Good to see you. Joshua (now Josh) Peterson

Mr. Towery Yesterday Carol Martin along with two older girls both teenagers beat Maria up. It was serious enough to call the police in. He tracked them down and gave them a severe warning. But Carol is being taken to Juvenile Court. The other girls at school have threatened to jump Maria. The police said if anything happens to get their names and he will pick them up. As long as Maria is at school she should get protected from these girls. I've told her if they bother her to go straight to you only. If anything happens to her in school, I will hold the school responsible. Talking to Carol on your part won't do any good. Thanks Mrs. Compton

Mrs. Allison, Please accept my apology for not seeing the progress report on Francisco dated 2-23. Since recently being granted custody of him and his sister Velma it has been a lot different dealing with their schooling on a day to day basis. Both of them have attitude problems and I think that is due to the fact that they have basically been with their mother most of the time. To make a long story short I assure you they are in a better environment with me. I know things don't happen over night but I will do my best to help Francisco try to reach the goal you and I would like for him to achieve. Thank you for being concerned and making it known to me what his strong and weak points are. As I have said before please accept my apology. I did not see the report until last night. By the way Francisco Gonzales Jr is his legal name. Vasquez is his mothers name. Thank you again for your time and effort in helping Francisco. Thank you Francisco Gonzales SR

The opening line of a sixth grade writing assignment on "What I Want to be When I Grow Up"... "When I am in my adultery...."

What I learned:

- **The job of the teacher in promoting basic language, written communication and spelling is truly critical.**
- **Field trips are popular and fun.**
- **What teachers and schools deal with is never ending, often surprising.**

Acknowledgements

I would especially like to thank and recognize Mr. Stephen Hillyard, my long time Assistant Principal for his listening ear, support and encouragement. He remains one of the finest teachers I have ever seen. I would also like to thank Mrs. Mary Stockstill, secretary, who stuck by me for twenty-nine years. Her love of children, respect for education, and care of our community made walking into our school a happy experience every day.

I recognize, appreciate and thank Mrs. Nellie Quander, my role model, a colleague principal and leader, example of compassion and excellence. Also, Dr. Herman Howard, Area Superintendent, who urged me to become Principal at Cameron School which thus set me on a thirty year journey far more wonderful than most people ever have the opportunity to experience.

I would like to honor my Elementary Principal, Miss Delma Lacy at Rudolph Elementary School in Washington DC who selected me as a sixth grader to be her "Student Assistant."

My appreciation is also extended to Superintendents, Dr. "Bud" Spillane, Dr. Daniel Domenech and Dr. Jack Dale who along with my Cluster Superintendent, Ms. Betsy Fenske, showed enough faith in my ability to allow me to have goats in the courtyard, take countless camping trips, and be involved in numerous outlandish activities that promoted learning, established an environment, and created a professional learning community.

Great appreciation is extended Louise Gibney, coach, teacher and editor for her support with the compilation of "Touched By A Child."